Size Doesn't Matter

The Popular Man Presents:

Size Doesn't Matter

The Short Man's Handbook Of Dating And Relationship Success

Jonathan Bennett and David Bennett

Cover design: Meg Syverud (megsyv.com)

The Popular Man logo: Natalie Howard (nhoward.com)

Body language model in chapter 21: Natalie Howard

Theta Hill Press

Lancaster, Ohio

thetahillpress.com

Medical Disclaimer

Information in this book is intended as an educational aid only. No information contained in this book should be construed as medical or psychological advice, diagnosis, or treatment. Readers should consult appropriate health professionals on any matter relating to their health and well-being, and before starting any health improvement program.

ISBN: 0615939473

ISBN-13: 978-0615939476

ACKNOWLEDGMENTS

SHOUT OUTS AND THANKS

Jonathan

I'd like to give a special shout out to my family. I'm grateful for their patience as I put the time and energy into writing this book. I'd also like thank my grandparents and parents, who taught me how to be popular while still having values.

Joshua Wagner deserves a special mention since he taught me a lot about humor, routines, and many other things. He was a great "model" from whom I learned a ton.

I also want to express my thanks to Dave Adams who always reminds me to stay on the right path and taught me many other valuable tips as well.

Finally, I want to thank Elizabeth Cobey-Piper and Susie Hardesty of "Dating Directions" and "Affinity Matchmaking" for all they've done. I also offer sincere thanks to Michol Childress and Luisa Canneto for their hard work in promoting our events and your insights.

David

I want to thank my wife Jennifer and daughter Elizabeth, and of course my parents Barry and Jeanne, and grandma Margie, for instilling in me a love of writing, teaching, and public speaking.

Joshua Wagner has been a great friend and inspiration. The many hours Jonathan, he and I spent coming up with various models of success helped make this project possible.

I'd also like to thank David Adams, who is always up for a fun night of relaxing and hanging out, sometimes around a fire.

Also, many thanks to Elizabeth Cobey-Piper and Susie Hardesty of "Dating Directions" and "Affinity Matchmaking," the best matchmakers in central Ohio, hands down. And to Michol Childress and Luisa Canneto for all your hard work and talent.

CONTENTS

Introduction

The State You Are In

"I would date you, but you're too short for me."

She tried to be really nice when she said it to me in seventh grade, even adding that it wasn't really my problem. It was hers. However, it really was my problem because I was the one experiencing the rejection. And, it was due to an issue I couldn't even change!

Every short guy on the planet has heard similar words or will hear them if he's actively trying to date women. It comes with the territory of being a short man in modern society.

However, there are two types of short guys in the world: those who let their height cripple them emotionally and those who transcend their alleged vertical inferiority and have a successful, fulfilled life (including with women). I used to be the first guy, but transformed myself into the second. Which are you now? Which do you want to be?

The first chapter will primarily deal with the struggles that come with being short. However, right now I want to talk about how I moved beyond the negativity of my short height and into a life of confidence and fulfillment.

When I was a kid, I was very popular, even though I was short. However, once I hit junior high, I became frustrated. I fit in well with people, but never had a clue how to get girls to like me. This frustration continued throughout college into my mid-twenties. I blamed my failures on many factors, but the biggest one of all was my height.

I felt frustrated and helpless in dating. If I wanted to lose weight, I consulted a weight loss book. If I needed to change my oil, I read a book about it or watched someone who knew how to do it. If I needed to learn physics, I studied it. Yeah, I'm going somewhere with this...

However, no one ever told me the truth about dating. I heard from parents and teachers that I just had to "be myself"- a nice, passive, friendly guy - and women would love me. Except women didn't like me, let alone love me. They typically passed me over for someone "bad for them," at least according to my standards, and their own self-professed standards. And, these guys were usually taller than I was.

I continued to try the same techniques over and over again just under different names and with a few subtle changes. This formula kept me very lonely (except a few dates and relationships I occasionally "lucked into"). But, I figured it had to work because I knew of no other options. I assumed I failed because I was short, even though there are short guys who date beautiful women. I just wasn't one of them!

Yet, I reached a point where I realized the way I approached attracting women was completely wrong. I began to watch successful guys in action. Some were shorter than I, yet they easily made friends and picked up hot women. I also studied the science of attraction and realized that looks (including height) were only part of the equation.

I remember moments from college when I absolutely hated myself. I had no dates, few friends, and felt frustrated to my very core. I woke up with no zeal for life and very little to look forward to.

Now, I have a great job, a thriving side business, lots of friends, and I get attention wherever I go. In fact, I'm usually the center of attention because I make it that way. As for the women, I get attention from lots of beautiful ladies. I'm married now, so I'm not in the market for them. But, I still get the attention. I have to turn them away. Isn't that a nice change from my previous state? Now I use the skills I've learned to help guys just like you date them instead.

Remember the two people I talked about earlier? Let's mention them again.

-Miserable, frustrated, and dateless short guy.

-Happy and successful short guy in a relationship.

Let's ask those questions again too: Which are you now? Which do you want to be?

You can be the second person. I've walked that journey and so have many other short men. It's not the easiest path and some people succeed more than others. However, being short is not a barrier to being happy and dating beautiful women. This book will give you the tips necessary to transform your life, if you're willing.

I encourage you to read each chapter slowly and apply the techniques taught within them. Do the assignments too. They're designed to get you out of your comfort zone. Reading this book won't change your life. Applying the techniques will. So, however mentally difficult an assignment may be, it's important to do it.

So, get to it! Start reading and even more importantly start acting. I would wish you luck, but, with these techniques you won't need luck. Even if you're short.

We have three sites we want you to visit to help you master the concepts in this book, and to get encouragement. First, thepopularman.com. There are over 200 free articles waiting for you there. Second, confidencedelivery.com. Sign up to get tips and motivational stories, like the ones in this book, delivered two to three times a week to your inbox. Get a free e-book too. Finally, go to verticalimpact.net. Here, you will find specific tips for shorter guys.

Chapter One

The Hard Facts Of Height

The first two chapters are going to be a little negative, so bear with me. I'm going to start by presenting some of the hard, unfortunate facts about being a short guy. I'm not doing it to be a downer. And, it's likely most readers have experienced a lot of what I mention anyway. But, I won't bring this this stuff up at all after Chapter 2 (except occasionally). I'm sharing this information so you can face up to the reality of being short, then overcome that reality and dominate life.

First, shorter guys are typically less successful in their careers. Taller men have been shown to make more money and receive more promotions. That's right, just for being tall, a guy can make more money than his short co-workers. One study found that, throughout his career, a tall man can make over $150,000 more than his shorter counterparts! This kind of discrepancy is more common in sales and management type positions, but it's still troubling (see apa.org/monitor/julaug04/standing.aspx).

Second, shorter guys don't do as well in political careers. For example, since 1900, the taller US presidential candidate has almost always won. In addition, the media sometimes ridicules shorter political leaders, like when French President Nicholas Sarkozy visited England and the media focused on his height instead of more pressing political issues. While you might not be interested in a political career, it's still galling to know you'd face discrimination if you were, just because you're a short man (see omg-facts.com/Interesting/Since-1900-The-Taller-Candidate-Has-Almo/53662).

Finally, let me confirm what every reader of this book probably already knows intuitively: women prefer taller men. Taller guys are more likely to be married and have more children. They are also viewed by women as more innately attractive and sexually powerful. In addition, ladies have a marked preference for taller men even when simply considering whom they will date. In other words, shorter guys are less likely to even be considered, let alone chosen, by women as dating partners (see shortsupport.org/Research/personals.html and jrscience.wcp.muohio.edu/Research/HumanNatureProgArticles/dontwantnoshortshortmanFI.html).

In one 1978 study by Graziano, Brothen, and Berscheid, women preferred guys of medium height (5′9″- 5′11″) to both shorter *and* taller guys. This perhaps shows that there may be a limit to the male height advantage in dating.

Obviously, these statistics are troubling for short guys. It's why some people have begun talking about "heightism," especially in Western societies like the United States and Europe. It's hard to deny that short men face a good deal of discrimination in society.

However, this discussion isn't really within the scope of this book. I am focused on improving you as a person and getting you dates. You can find more about the "heightism" discussion on the internet.

But, I do want to add that one of the best ways to combat bias against short men is for short men to prove the stereotypes wrong. That's why this book is concerned with creating high value, confident, and successful short men. The more of us that gain respect and credibility, the more the stereotypes about height will shatter.

So, I've established that short guys have it more difficult in work, politics, and dating. I'm sure that I'm not telling you anything you didn't already know. But, here's what I want you to take out of this chapter:

First, you have an inherent social disadvantage.

You can overcome this, which is what this book is about. However, don't be surprised if, at times, people will use your height against you when you're practicing the techniques in this book. Don't worry; I have some great responses in "Appendix B."

Second, you'll have to work harder.

We all have disadvantages in dating. Being short is one of those. And, it's one you can't change. The fat guy can get his butt to the gym. The unemployed loser can get a job. The short guy can…well…not exactly grow taller. So, you'll have to bust your butt to be socially desirable and superior in other ways.

So, keep these in mind. I'm not going to mention height discrimination anymore. While others can and should work to change society's perception of short men, that crusade doesn't help you get dates in the present. I, on the other hand, want to get you dates…right now.

Your assignment for today is to vow that you're going to put in the hard work necessary to change your life for the better, especially when it comes to dating. Really make a strong commitment. Lots of people say they're going to change, but stop when it gets tough. You be the exception to the rule. Change your life and finally find true love and happiness.

Chapter Two

Venting Time

When I was a senior in high school, I was really, really nice to a freshman girl in the hopes of getting her to go to Homecoming with me. This strategy never works…but I digress. I let her share my locker (hers was all the way on the third floor), let her drive my car (yeah, she was fourteen), and went out of my way to make her high school transition easier.

When I finally asked her to Homecoming (in a very weak way), she became somewhat flustered, clearly shocked that I wanted more than just friendship. She responded that she was simply too tall for me and it would be awkward.

In other words, I was too short.

Does this story make you angry? Does it make you sad? Does it get your brain working overtime as you think of all the times you've been rejected by women because of height (or any reason that you secretly have suspected is height-related)?

All nice and worked up? Now it's your time to share your stories. But, this isn't a time for a "pity party" or "bitch-fest," like so many alleged places that provide short support. I want you to do this so that you can get your feelings out and move past them.

Research by Candace Pert (summarized in her book Molecules of Emotion) shows that we can actually become addicted to bad emotions in the same way we can become addicted to a drug or another bad habit. It sounds crazy, doesn't it? Why would anyone want to feel a bad emotion? Well, why would anyone want to use meth even though it has destroyed his life? It's called an addiction for a reason.

Many people are so used to bad emotions that their brain actually becomes wired to expect and even crave bad, but familiar, emotions. And, when they don't get those feelings, they have to go out and experience (or, even worse, create) negative emotions to feel "normal" again. It's like a junkie seeking a heroin fix.

If you secretly felt good or pleased to hear my rejection story, even if in some perverse way, then you might be addicted to the negativity that can come from always getting the short end of the stick in life (pun intended).

You probably don't like it and genuinely want better for yourself. But, the self-loathing and negativity have just become too familiar to you. So, your brain constantly seeks out horror stories of short people facing rejection. Then, you happily pile on your own examples, creating a crippling feedback loop.

It has to stop right now. Negative people (in the bitter, whiny sense) are rarely admired in society and they even more rarely get dates. I can promise you this: no woman (at least a high-value one) wants to spend a date hearing about your height rejection stories. A girl will likely listen to you out of politeness, but you'll never get close to having anything romantic or physical with her.

Now, I want you to get all of your stories off your chest. Write them down, tell them to someone, share them on the Internet, whatever. Don't try too hard to dredge up forgotten memories. You likely have more than enough seared into your brain ready for instant recall. Vocalize them or write them down. This is part of your assignment.

Now, destroy them. Kidding. I want you to keep them. They are good "before" stories of how you failed with women to laugh about later when you're a dating beast. But, put them away for now. Out of sight and out of mind. They're not even good motivation.

Sure, they might have motivated you to pick up this book, which is good. However, from this point forward, let your motivation be the person you're going to become. Your reason for being isn't rejection, anger, loneliness, disappointment and frustration. From this point, it's going to be acceptance, happiness, fulfillment, attractiveness, and having a relationship. Let your pursuit of these be your guiding principle.

For the second part of your assignment, write down all the positive emotions you'll be feeling once you start dating the women of your dreams (on a separate sheet). Let these be your motivation and inspiration from this point forward.

Chapter Three

You Can't Change Your Height, But You Can Change Your Mind

The internet is full of fun websites with optical illusions, which illustrate how our brains constantly trick us. One way the brain plays tricks is to adjust our perception of reality. It alters, without us even being aware of it, what we see in an attempt to make the best possible sense of the signals we receive from the world. In other words, the brain is always "filling in the blanks" based on expectations and other factors.

This can work with emotional states, as well. We live our lives according to our mental and emotional maps of the world. Put another way, everything we see and experience is interpreted through our overall mindset. It's the same as traveling from Florida to Maine. There are many different ways to get there, some with better results than others. Traveling over interstates will probably lead to better outcomes (like quicker arrival time, less car wear and tear, etc.) than going on dirt roads.

The same is true of our mental and emotional maps. We process life's experiences based on those maps. These have been formed over many years and some are genetic. And, many maps are simply unhelpful. They lead to misery and unhappiness, much like the rushed traveler whose map from Florida to Maine lacks the interstates.

Let me give you an example of a map of the world. A young lady grows up poor and has no father. She never learns social interaction with men and is constantly seeking attention. She hits puberty. She sleeps with many different men who use her only for sex. But, in spite of the problems associated with this, and all the advice of friends, she continues dating the very jerks who constantly mistreat her.

She does this because it's her map of the world. Just like a map that has only dirt roads, her map only reflects her negative experiences with men (starting with her dad and continuing in a spiral). She doesn't form a meaningful relationship with a good man because it's not on her map. She may not even be able to be attracted to a stable and civil guy, since she has known so few of them.

You probably have a map of the world that tells you "short guys can't get dates." If that's been your experience, then how could you be expected to believe any differently? So, when people tell you that short guys can get dates, you don't believe them. They're telling you to take a different route when you can't even see those roads on your map!

We've talked about the importance of change and its difficulty. Well, today you're going to change one of the most difficult aspects of all: your mindset, or your emotional and mental map of the world. Starting today you're going to begin to change the way you perceive the world and how you present yourself.

Your mindset is not only mental, but also physical. It's physically embedded into your brain through wiring. It is why, when you see a beautiful girl, you might feel frustrated and anxious even though you haven't even consciously thought about her or her rejecting you. But, your brain immediately associates a pretty woman with rejection!

That's brain wiring at work, and the connection between "women" and "rejection" is explained by Hebb's Rule, which states that neurons in the brain that fire together, wire together. Thus two associations can literally be wired together in the physical brain. Changing such an embedded association requires some work.

So, if a girl grows up associating male love with her dad's horrible treatment of her, then the neurons related to both become wired together in the brain. Thus, whenever the neurons for "love" fire, so do the neurons for "totally mean jerks that mistreat me."

Hebb's rule also explains why even though your aunt has been a sweet old lady for the last ten years, your brain still associates her with nasty comments she made to you when you were ten, so whenever you see her, your first reaction is anger and resentment. It is because the neurons for "aunt" are wired with the neurons for "anger and resentment."

Scientists used to believe your brain wiring was set in stone by the time you turned twenty-five. After that, you couldn't change it much. Fortunately, we now know that's not the case. Research by Dr. Jeffrey Schwartz (See his books You Are Not Your Brain and The Mind and the Brain) and others shows that the brain is plastic, meaning it can change. This changing of brain wiring, or neuroplasticity, is very important for short guys. It means we can get over our hang-ups at any age.

Changing your brain is easy right? Sure! If you're a toddler or possibly a teen. Otherwise, it's not terribly easy. But, it is possible and that's all that matters. I'm going to put you on the two-part plan to change your brain. And, it works. I've used it and it's helped many of my clients (of all heights) get over their hang-ups.

The first is a mental trick. You're basically going to play with your mind and convince it of certain things. Weird? Maybe. However, you let others convince your mind of certain things all the time. So, why not listen to yourself instead? You do this by using affirmations and declarations.

As I cover more thoroughly in the book Say It Like You Mean It: How To Use Affirmations and Declarations To Create The Life You

Want (co-written with David), affirmations are statements of intent describing who you want to be and/or what you want to accomplish. You say these out loud or listen to others saying them. The point behind them is that they are positive self-talk to counteract your negative brain wiring.

It sounds hokey (and maybe a little weird), but it can work. The key is to be consistent and keep up with your affirmations even when you're not quite feeling all that positive. Over time, you will start to actually believe what you're saying and start to live it. It may not seem like it at first, but you have to give it time. Trust me on this one.

I'd recommend using the language of process when creating affirmations. For example, if you want to get a date, write, "I am attracting beautiful women on a date" rather than "I am dating beautiful women." Your brain knows you're not dating beautiful women, so it will automatically send out negative thoughts reminding you what BS your current affirmation is. It can't do this to you as much when you employ process language (because it's somewhat future oriented).

The other side of mental practice is declarations. These are statements of intent declaring who you want to be and what you want to do. They're easy to write; you're only crafting statements of intention that express action. Using the previous theme, you could write, "I commit to take all the necessary steps to date beautiful women." Use the language of commitment for best results.

Make all your affirmations and declarations positive. In other words, don't say what you're *not* going to be or do, but rather what you are going to become or do. For example, if you want to lose weight, don't say, "I am losing weight." You're just putting the word (and idea of gaining) "weight" in your brain.

Say instead, "I'm attracting a fit and healthy body that women desire." Put "fit," "healthy," "desire," and "women" into your subconscious mind instead of weight.

Your assignment is to write a set of affirmations and declarations. The first step is to come up with several goals. This doesn't have to be just dating goals. Add in anything you'd like to become or do, like work success, social advancement, and making money.

Give this list some serious thought. It's going to form the foundation for your life transformation.

Next, take your goals and craft them into affirmations. Do the same with declarations. Make sure to use process in your affirmations and include action in your declarations. And, use positive language in both. Here are some examples:

<u>Affirmations</u>

- I am attracting a well-paying job with benefits and flexibility.

- I am becoming the center of attention wherever I go.

- I am developing the ability to approach and close with all women.

Declarations

- I commit to pursue a well-paying job with benefits and flexibility.

- I commit to be the center of attention everywhere.

- I commit to approach and close with every woman I meet and find attractive.

Then, you'll need to say them every single day for the duration of this book (and beyond). I recommend getting into a meditative space and mindset, then just say them out loud. Breathe in and out and make it a relaxing time. It's helpful to say your declarations first thing in the morning to start your day off right.

The second way to change your map of the world is through action. This is through practice, practice, practice. Yes, your coaches (band director, etc.) were right. It's important to practice what you preach (to yourself). This is especially vital because practice is the best way to weaken old and unhelpful brain wiring and associations (such as "hot woman=rejection of me"), and create new, more helpful ones (such as "hot woman=time to approach confidently and be successful").

Basically, you must hold your affirmations and declarations in your mind while taking steps to achieve them daily. So, if you've committed to losing weight, then make sure that your actual choices reflect that. In this case, you'd practice eating healthily and working out.

The practice is the difficult part. However, it can be done. The second part of your assignment is to take your goals that you turned into affirmations and declarations and write out a few action steps to achieve those goals.

As an example, if you picked attracting a well-paying job, write beneath it: go to college, submit new resumes, etc. However, only choose steps that are helpful. For the dating goals, your action-step right now can simply be "read and follow this book." I'll be giving you plenty of actionable tips (and assignments) down the line!

Now it's time to start changing your mindset. This chapter may only seem to have a slight connection to dating, but it's very important. If you have the wrong mindset, then you'll only sabotage yourself in the near future. These affirmations and declarations are laying the mental foundation for the changes you are going to make in the rest of the book.

CHAPTER FOUR

ATTRACTION 101

I went through a period of my life when I went to the gym every day. I was one of the "regulars" and worked hard at sculpting my body and staying in shape. Lots of other "regulars" did the same. Most of us were single and, judging by the conversations, we were there for the same reason: getting in shape to get girls to fall for us. Yet, the majority of us stayed perpetually single. We got in great shape, which was a plus, but the women didn't exactly start flocking to our ripped biceps and squat-strengthened legs.

While working out and being fit are great (and important), we were all ignorant of the basic principles of attraction. We thought (incorrectly) that spending hours in the gym sculpting the perfect body would win us adoring throngs of women who would be begging to date us.

Ignorance of the rules of attraction is extremely commonplace, not just among gym rats. Most guys have no idea what women look for in a guy. Do you have a guess? Did you say good looks? Wrong. Treat them like a queen? Hell no. Good personality? Kind of. How about power, protection, and dominance? If you said any of those, you are correct.

Women are biologically programmed to like dominant men. Throughout history, females have been the weaker sex. They needed provided for and protected from dangers. Their brains are still wired for that basic need. It's why even a seemingly independent female still craves a relationship with cocky unemployed bad boy over a stable, but boring accountant.

You see, those cocky bad boys, in spite of their faults, often come across as dominant and capable of providing and protecting. You might be a really nice guy, but are you capable of protecting her, whether physically or in other ways? Maybe, but being "nice" doesn't guarantee it. In fact, being too nice might even disqualify you in the protection department. This is why so many "nice" guys end up as "just friends."

In today's culture, dominance isn't necessarily about fighting ability, although women love those types of guys too (athletes, jerks, etc.). Dominance exists any time a guy has power. This explains why females love bosses, rich men, teachers, and other men in positions of power. And, it's why ladies prefer tall guys. All things considered, tall guys present (initially) as more dominant than short ones.

Men typically look at physical characteristics when evaluating the attractiveness of females. So, they assume women focus primarily on physical traits as well. Women do value good looks. However, a man's dominance and power (or lack thereof) are far more important in a woman's attraction (or not) to a man.

You might think I'm joking, but many scientific studies show dominance and confidence are more important than looks when attracting a woman. One recent study by Hill, Hunt, et. al., published in the journal Evolution and Human Behavior, confirmed this.

However, even if you don't necessarily believe the science, look at the world around you if you need more proof. Do you think Hugh Hefner gets girls a third of his age because he's handsome? Do the fifty-something CEOs mess around with the hot secretary because they're in perfect shape? Did that 97-year old dude get Anna Nicole Smith (a 1990s model) because he had perfectly styled hair? "Hell no" is the answer to all these questions!

This should actually be good news to short men. No check that. This is amazing, awesome, spectacular, life-changing news. You can't alter your height. However, you can work on being more dominant and project to women how you are capable of providing for and protecting them.

All of those guys mentioned previously had power (and the attention of women) for one reason: they're valuable. Thus, the goal of all men looking for a date should be to attain high-value in the eyes of women. If you are highly valued, you become powerful (by virtue of your value) and attractive. Powerful, high-value guys push basic attraction buttons in women on a subconscious level. You still have to do the work of interaction and winning them over, but it's much easier when they're practically salivating over you at the start.

Let's look at the previous examples. Hugh Hefner is rich and famous and achieved it through a popular business. He has clear value and power. In today's society, wealth makes you an obvious provider and protector. Those CEOs are leaders at the top of the pyramid. And, they're also usually wealthier. The same is the case with the oil tycoon who married Anna Nicole Smith. These are not average guys.

However, thanks to understanding the science of attraction, it is easy to make certain adjustments to the way you act, speak, think, etc., so women subconsciously perceive you as higher value, even if in reality you aren't a CEO or rich athlete.

So, let's review what makes a man attractive to women. It basically comes down to power and dominance. You must show her that you are a high-value man who is capable of power and dominance (or that you're actually powerful and dominant).

Looks do matter. However, they're more demonstrative of a man's high-value than an essential trait in and of themselves. That's why a guy can be an overweight musician and still get the girls while a timid, backward fitness freak can be perpetually lonely.

The converse of this, of course, means that there are also guys who are unattractive because they fail to push those primal attraction buttons. These guys are weak, submissive, and boring. They don't show women they can provide and protect and they have little value to women outside of being "just friends." These are the typical "nice guys" who succeed in some ways, but really do finish last with women.

I am guessing that most people reading this book fit into the "nice guy" category. You may even be offended that attraction doesn't favor you. But, face facts. How many times have you, a nice guy, lost out to a guy who, by most definitions, was a bad person, but had cockiness and rebellion in his favor? Rebels may annoy you, but they sure as hell come across as dominant and powerful with the ability to provide and protect (even if it's just a mirage).

I have no desire to create jerks and bad boys. However, I will be teaching you many ways to be assertive, confident, and high-value. You're not going to become a jerk unless you want to (please don't). But the squishy, boring "nice guy" is going out the window too. Tell him goodbye because he's leaving today. Be sure to thank me for it later!

Before you object, just ask yourself a couple of questions. First, have you been a nice guy, or an assertive one, throughout your life? Likely, if you're reading this, you fit the passive, nice guy stereotype (or are close to it). So, here is the next question: how is that working out for you? Has being the nice guy helped you get dates and be the best person you can be? Not likely or you wouldn't even have purchased this book.

Trust me; I used to be the "nice guy." I thought it would get me dates, but in the end, it just made me the "shoulder to cry on" when women were having trouble with their bad-boy boyfriends. Let me reiterate gentlemen: being the nice, passive, and always-agreeable guy *hasn't worked for you.* I know I am repeating myself, but for many guys it is hard to let this side of you die, even if it *never* works for you.

So, in summary, quit thinking that attraction is only about looks. Focus on value! Not only is value something you can increase (unlike height), you can even do it in a fairly short period of time. Oh, and like the bad boys, you can even fake it in the beginning. But, you definitely will have to raise your value or project it better if you want dates, especially lots of them with beautiful women.

When I was in middle school, I beat a rather difficult boss character in *Super Mario Brothers 2* for the Nintendo. I told others about my accomplishment and guess what? No one cared. I was appalled because it was a difficult task and I thought it was a worthwhile accomplishment. But, what I thought didn't matter.

You'll have to develop traits and accomplishments that are considered universally valued. Oh, and before you ask, yes, being tall fits this category, at least in American and European culture. So are being thin and having nice eyes. And there are many, many more.

The next several chapters are dedicated to identifying valuable traits and accomplishments, then helping you achieve them.

Your assignment for this chapter is simple. Stop believing the myths about attraction and embrace the truth. It's harder than you think because you've been conditioned to keep trying the same old methods over and over again ("be yourself," "go to the gym," "be nice," etc.). Just remember next time you're tempted to go back to the old ways: they've kept you single and frustrated all these years.

Chapter Five

Increase Your Wealth

In the last chapter, I gave a few examples of ugly guys getting stunningly beautiful women. In case you didn't notice, those dudes all had one trait going for them. If you were observant, you probably saw that they are or were filthy rich. And, yes, the stereotype holds completely true: women love wealthy guys.

My business works with the biggest matchmaking organization in the Columbus, Ohio area. The owners tell us an interesting, but unsurprising, fact about nearly all of their most beautiful female clients: they set an income minimum for guys they will consider dating. While they might deviate from that for the right guy, most of them definitely want a man who has some money. It's about providing and protecting, remember? In modern times, you don't have to hunt to provide, but you at least need some cash.

It's not only a dating thing either. Rich people are highly valued in almost every society. The United States and Europe are no exceptions. In fact, we Westerners are typically even more affluence obsessed. Those with nice cars, beautiful homes, and luxury items win the respect and admiration of others, even if they are total scumbags in other ways.

Don't get too discouraged, since short of being born wealthy, it's very rare to get filthy rich especially in the span of reading a book. But, I want to include this chapter for a couple of reasons. First, it really is a value indicator and it's worth talking about. Second, wealth is relative. This means the more money you get, the more high-value you can be. So, these tips should help you at least make more money.

Here's an example of why even being slightly richer gives you an advantage with women. An average guy at a club is competing with another average guy for the attention of a hot girl. All things being equal, one says, "Let's take my Corvette over to my condo so we can sit in my hot tub for a while." The other one says, "Let's take my Civic over to my studio apartment to sit on my futon for a while." I think you know where this is going (or where the girl is going).

Making more money isn't terribly easy in the current economy. But, there is one thing you can do to at least make an attempt: effort. Sadly, a lot of men today simply lack motivation to be successful and make money. While money should never be the primary motivator in anyone's life, you need at least some money to date women and live a moderately fulfilling life.

While some people may say they don't care about money, every one of them would gladly take a ten thousand dollar handout in a second. They just don't care about working for money. And, that's okay, as long as they're not mooching off of me. Still, if a guy wants to date beautiful women, he'll at least need some cash to take them out. Get more cash and he'll impress them enough that they might want to date him even more (although as a rule, never try to "buy" the love of a woman through gifts, etc.).

The first way to make more money is obvious. Get a job. Or get another one. Or pick up more hours. I know this may not always be possible, but it's more possible than you think. Being unemployed and living in your parents' house is very low-value. Telling a girl you're taking her back to your "room" when you're twenty-eight just makes you look like a loser.

So, even if you go out and get a service job and start saving to get an apartment, it's better than having nothing. Saying, "I work at McDonald's" is still preferable to "I don't work and live with my parents." Obviously, having a good job is even more brag-worthy, which brings us to the next point…

Find a way to get a better job, whether it's applying to different places or going back to school. Plus, you can tell women you're a student, which is better than being unemployed or not looking for a job. Start the process quickly because it's easy to get stuck in a dead-end job. And pick useful classes. Studying history may be interesting, but it'll keep you working at Starbucks (trust me on this one).

Another way to get money is to sell some of your stuff. It will be temporary money, but it might be better than keeping a bunch of crap you don't use around. And, maybe you can use the money to invest in yourself by following some of the suggestions in this book that require money. Better to give your money to bettering yourself than bettering someone else's bottom line. However, *never* sell prized possessions to take a woman out for an expensive meal, buy her expensive jewelry, etc., especially if you barely know her. That may work in the movies, but it won't make a woman become attracted to you in real life.

You can also make money by spending less of it. Cut back on non-essentials and save in other ways. Use less water when you shower, eat generic brand food, turn off the lights when you leave the room, double up on your errands to save gas, and so on. Don't be a cheapskate, but these tips will save some of your money to be used to better yourself and spend when you go out seeking dates. The corporate bigwigs at the electric company don't need your date money anyway.

Finally, consider starting your own business. I recommend this for a couple reasons. First, if it succeeds you are the primary one making money. You take the risk, but you keep most of the reward. Second, it puts you in a leadership position (see the next chapter).

When I go out, people love when I talk about my business. It's very interesting and unusual, which helps, but men and women also find it interesting because it shows I'm in charge of something valued (business). So, I have the advantage of extra money and extra attention when I'm out. And, when I share what I do, the attention leads to more money because lots of them buy my stuff. It's not a bad deal at all, is it?

This book isn't about starting a business, so I'm not going to say much about the technical details. Obviously, your first step will be to come up with a viable business idea. I'd recommend reading Millionaire Fastlane by MJ Demarco. He's a cool guy who has been insanely successful. He shares great tips for you to find success. He cuts through the traditional advice that either doesn't work or gets you rich so slowly that you will likely die before you can enjoy it.

I'm not a wealthy man like the other examples I've given. But, I do pretty well through a combination of all of the above methods. I got a better job a few years ago, work overtime if I'm able, teach at a college part-time, and make money through my writing, speaking and consulting business. In addition, I re-use towels, turn off my lights, and have instituted other money saving tips around my house. It is possible to do better financially if you really try.

For your assignment, I'd like you to come up with a list of ways you're going to get more money. Make it concrete and add in action steps. It's important that you don't just talk the talk, but walk the walk. Change is tough, but remember, shorty, you have to do everything else right. A woman will make exceptions for a tall, bad-boy with no money. But, a short guy who lives with his parents? I personally wouldn't take that risk.

So, while you may not be Hugh Hefner or Donald Trump, if you can at least show that you are a good provider and protector and occasionally flash some bling, you'll be at a big competitive advantage, even against all those taller guys.

CHAPTER SIX

GET THEM LOOKING UP TO YOU

I wasn't always popular and successful. In fact, there were moments in my life when I was in quite a terrible rut. However, one life event changed all that: becoming a teacher. It allowed me to bring out the latent popularity that I had let stay dormant for many years. And, I became extremely popular at my school. Students followed me around and treated me like I was a celebrity.

I was just beginning to hone my skills at that time, but I had an instant popularity boost just by being their teacher. Why? Leadership. It was my room and I was in charge. Look at it this way. I was the center of attention every day. I called the shots. I held their futures in my hands. I received their friendship and respect. Students frequently confessed their admiration of my swagger and occasionally even their crushes on me. Remember from Attraction 101: it's all about the power.

Now, you might think this doesn't describe most teachers or many of yours. That's because most teachers squander their leadership potential by resorting to force instead of inspiration or they're just bland individuals who lack personality. Yet, those teachers who inspire, lead, and bond with their students? They're often role models for life and receive more attention than they know what to do with!

The moral of this story? Do you want to be popular and date beautiful women? Then, you'll need to get yourself into leadership positions. Being a leader gives you a huge advantage in the dating game because you are showing women that you have power and you can provide and protect. After all, you're organizing and leading others. Also, the more powerful the leader becomes, the better his chances with women. Don't believe me? Read up on the legendary sexual exploits of President Kennedy.

Also, having valuable traits and accomplishments is rare, and we humans know it. It's basic supply and demand. It's why a diamond ring is more valuable than a plastic spoon. The same is true when winning over women. You want to cultivate traits and seek accomplishments that set you apart from the rest. Just like with being rich, true leadership is pretty rare. Have it, and it sets you apart as high-value.

Most people go with the flow in the world and follow those in leadership positions. A man who takes charge and attracts followers isn't common. For example, many more people follow professional sports than actually play for the teams. There are 525 members of Congress and one President for three hundred million US residents. The same is true of successful musicians. Think about the last concert you attended. There may been five or six people on stage, but thousands in the audience. Get the picture?

If you can take a leadership position, proving you're more than just a typical follower, you'll be instantly more powerful and create greater value. The larger leadership position you can take, the more power and value you'll have.

You can approach becoming a leader in two ways. The first is to find existing leadership positions and try to fill them. For example, maybe you're a member of a civic or charitable group or are thinking of advancing at work. Or perhaps you've been involved with a club for a while and want to run for some type of office. Step up and seek these leadership positions.

The upside is that the positions are already available and you have a support system in place to help you as a leader. In addition, if you're already a member or employee of an organization, you should have (hopefully) earned some level of trust with others in the group. The downside of this path is that you have to be chosen, whether for a promotion or an elected position. If you're reading this book, you've likely been overlooked for a reason.

However, this path is the quickest one and assuming leadership in established groups and companies generally raises your prestige. Do it if you can.

The second, and typically best, option is to create leadership roles for yourself. Form a club or charitable group. Start a business. Found an underground newspaper or create a unique website. Whatever option you take, find a way to come up with leadership opportunities where you don't have to rely on others to put you in charge, but can attract organic followers through your excellence.

Be warned, though. You'll want to form a group or start a business with a couple of things in mind. First, make sure that your idea will actually bring you followers. Once again, the more potential followers, the better. Starting a local chapter of the "Klingon Language Society" might not win you many dates. Second, make sure that you can actually be a leader. You definitely don't want to start a group then watch as others take the glory (or it falls apart). Fortunately, some of the other chapters in this book will help you develop the necessary confidence to lead.

The upside of starting your own group or business is that you don't need to be recognized by others to become a leader. We addressed the downside in the last paragraph. But, even if you have a great idea and are a good leader, it's still a lot of work to successfully start anything from scratch. Nonetheless, building a great organization from the bottom-up makes you look really powerful and successful, if you can pull it off.

Your assignment for this chapter is to go through and list your current work and social situations. Then, I'd like you to outline ways you can take on more of a leadership role in these environments. Also, brainstorm a few business or other venture ideas where you could be the founder and leader. Don't forget to make your ideas something that others would actually enjoy (and women would find admirable).

Chapter Seven

Confidence Is King

As mentioned earlier, I was an extremely popular high school teacher. This experience started my study of popularity and social skills. I basically ran my room the way I felt like it and had the confidence to back it up. One day a student, who was extremely popular himself, told me, "Mr. Bennett walks around here like he owns the school." He meant it as a compliment and he was right.

I didn't own the school, but I might as well have because the students treated me like I did. And, I accomplished it all through the most highly valued trait in men. Can you guess what it is? If you said "confidence" then you get a gold star (and likely a date if you can develop it yourself).

Let's face it, a guy who has high self-esteem and a sense of confidence projects power and dominance to the world (even if he doesn't have it). And, there is evidence that our mindset about what we attempt actually affects whether or not we fail or succeed (see enpc.fr/ceras/compte/confidence.pdf).

Thus, if you're acting like you're confident, you're more likely to actually achieve what you're confident about. In other contexts, it's called "fake it 'til you make it." So, while I didn't actually own the school, because I acted like I did, the students picked up on it and treated me as if the building's deed read "Property of Jonathan Bennett." The other teachers, however, didn't get the same level of admiration and popularity. They acted like they were just…teachers.

A lot of short guys have a sense of self-esteem that lies somewhere between the toilet and the sewer. They were usually short boys, short toddlers, and small babies. Thus, short guys have been conditioned to believe that we are weak and unworthy (in sports, relationships, etc.). And, lots of short guys have become timid "yes" men with low self-worth as adults. That's pretty much the opposite of confidence…which women love, remember? So, get cracking on the confidence.

I already know the objections, so you don't have to even think (or say) them. One is that you can't have confidence because you're short and beaten down. Well, I'm short and was beaten down. Now, I do what I want and am respected and admired by women and men alike.

So do other short guys, famous and not so famous, who dominate in their jobs and social and romantic lives.

But, you say you don't want to become a cocky jerk. Well, guess what? Jerks get ladies! But, still I don't want you to turn into a jerk. If you are a shy, timid nice guy, what you think is cocky may actually be just run-of-the-mill confidence. You're not going to turn into a jerk unless you want to be a jerk.

If you have any other excuses or objections as to why you can't be confident, then get over them right now. If you want to get dates, you'll have to start believing in yourself and telegraphing that to others.

First, go out and think you're amazing, height and all. That means every morning you need to wake up and believe that you are going to conquer the day. From the second you get up, you'll have to counter your automatic feelings of inadequacy that your subconscious brain is chucking at you all the time. And, believe me, it will send out those feelings, especially at the start of your journey to personal change.

One way to start building your self-confidence immediately is to add something really cocky to your affirmations and declarations. Include a line like "I am developing more swagger every day," or "I commit to be the most awesome person in every room." And, start acting like it. It won't instantly make you a cocky bastard, but it's at least going to help stop those negative automatic thoughts.

Second, start racking up some real accomplishments. Learn to play an instrument. Complete a mud run like the Tough Mudder. Get a better job. Win an award. Learn a new skill. You can't simply raise self-esteem by telling yourself you're awesome (although that's a good start). You'll actually have to go out and have a reason to be cocky. Start achieving those accomplishments now.

Yeah, I'm short. But, I also own my own business, am active in public speaking, have a great job, have written several books, possess a Master's degree, teach college, finished two Tough Mudders, and am funny and intelligent. Am I cocky? Hell yes I am. It's because I have accomplishments. Do I get crap occasionally about my height? Sure. But, then the conversation moves towards my excellence and my height becomes irrelevant. Oh, and both men and women absolutely love my cocky attitude.

Third, a major component of confidence is not caring what others think. In fact, that's cockiness to a "T." A cocky guy simply doesn't care about the negative opinions of others. The biggest problem I see out of my short clients is they care what others think, almost to a fault. Someone they've never met calls them short and they flip out and dwell on it for weeks! That's not confidence, but its total opposite: insecurity.

We spend a whole chapter on detachment (see Chapter 9), but the gist of it can be summed up as: you have to stop worrying what others think. If someone calls you "short" or bashes you, you show them you simply don't care. Or you throw back a witty response. It makes you look strong and cocky and earns you both respect and admiration.

Fourth, there's the tip I referenced in this chapter's opening story: "act like you own the place." It's actually pretty easy. Everywhere you go, you just act like you're the owner. Most people are relaxed and in charge of their own spaces, like their cars or their homes. Even if you're not, then look at a business owner. He's in charge of that venue. He can hire and fire, kick out, invite, and should have no trouble talking to people. It's his place!

When you walk in anywhere, act like you own the place. Don't go around telling people that, of course. However, in your mind, determine that a space is yours. You own it. And, actually try to own the space (socially anyway). I always love this trick, especially when I am the center of attention and the actual owner comes up hoping to start a conversation with me.

If that trick doesn't quite do it, tell yourself, "I'm the shit" or something similar. You can laugh when you do it, but say it anyway. Build yourself up and get that confidence soaring through the roof. I talk more about confident body language later (see Chapter 20) that complements this section perfectly. But, even if you have to "fake it 'til you make it" at least you're projecting confidence to others. After a while, you'll start to feel the confidence that you're projecting.

For your assignment, I want you to list your accomplishments. They need to be fairly recent (or enduring, like a college degree). They also need to be valued by large segments of society. So, that one time you won honorable mention at the third grade field day doesn't count. You'll likely have more accomplishments than you think.

Be proud of these! Don't go out and brag about them constantly, but let them undergird a basic sense of confidence that you nurture. Second, write out a few goals that you would like to achieve. Make sure they are realistically achievable, but also valuable. If you've always wanted to write a book or screenplay or anything else, put it down. Then, start working on those goals right now!

I'd also like you to go out somewhere and act like you own the place. Do it with a friend or group of friends if possible. Remember, it's acting, so go out and try it. Give yourself permission for a period of time and see how it changes the way you think and act.

Chapter Eight

Be A Damn Man

There is some genuine hatred of short men out there. Of course, there's hatred of every group of people in the world. Just ask any minority. But, it doesn't mean it hurts any less when it's directed our way. One way that people attack short guys is by questioning our very manhood, which is why a term we often hear thrown around is "manlet." There is nothing worse than implying we're not even one hundred percent dude.

Let me contrast this "manlet" bullshit with a little bio of my former karate instructor. The guy is a black-belt and tough as nails. He is probably under 5′3″ but is solid muscle. I was told he could bench press over 250 pounds and I believe it. He would go against taller guys in karate competitions and literally beat the crap out of them. I'm sure that anyone (of any height) who called him a "manlet" would not only find out who was the real man in that debate, but also instantly regret it (while lying on the pavement).

Another shorter guy who is tough as nails is Damian Ross, the head of the "Self Defense Company." His business offers self-defense training that my business uses and recommends to clients. If you see this guy in action, you would know he is more "man" than most tall guys.

As short guys, we are a real disadvantage in the whole masculine stereotype business and aren't taken as seriously as men. Women typically like a rugged, fighter type of guy who is tall, dark, and handsome. And, men try to emulate that guy. Or, at least Hollywood and other parts of popular culture tell us we should. Also, the prototypical leader, whether in politics or in business, is a "take names and kick ass" kind of guy.

This is probably why studies show that shorter men make less money in their careers and get fewer dates. We aren't perceived as naturally masculine enough to warrant either career advancement or a chance at love. We're viewed more as adult children than men. It doesn't always result in bullying or rejection. Sometimes it leads to pity. Of course, no one wants that either!

Although these facts are depressing, there are fortunately ways to be more masculine that don't involve growing taller or having to become a black belt in karate. Although, if you are younger and have the discipline to do it, a black belt certainly would help!

First, manliness is often related to having accomplishments that are considered masculine. I guarantee that no one would consider an MMA fighter girly, even if he liked to wear pink in the ring. It's because successfully fighting other guys (and being famous for doing it) is considered a manly trait.

If you do manly things, you'll also be regarded as more manly, even if you carry yourself in a generally less than manly way (although you can be more successful if you do both). What are some manly accomplishments? Basically, we've already discussed most of them when we talked about value in the previous chapters.

If you can become a leader, be funny, act confidently, find success in various endeavors, etc. you will be perceived as being more of a man. It's like with my karate instructor. Anyone who knew him had no doubt about his manliness. Those who didn't know and implied he wasn't a real man, quickly discovered otherwise. Start cultivating your valuable skills and find some genuine self-esteem. If you're not starting to live up to your potential as a high-value man, re-read the previous chapters.

Second, manliness is often a matter of attitude. Are you a passive, people-pleasing "nice guy," or do you stand up for yourself and take risks? You have to develop the attitude that you are masculine. It's not a tough-guy act (because they're often weak blowhards), but it does involve keeping the attitude of a provider and protector.

Try to keep that mentality throughout your entire day. While you don't have to be rescuing helpless women from burning buildings (there are professionals to do that), you should, on a regular basis, be developing that mindset. And, make your choices based on that mindset.

So, let's say you're at work and the office bully is picking on another employee. What would a provider and protector do? You're out with friends and a girl seems like she's lost. What would a provider and protector do? Get yourself in the mindset of a powerful, courageous man and then act accordingly. You'll come across as a real man who can be an asset to your employer and be valuable to women as well.

If you are genuinely scared or lack the skills to back up your confident words, sign up for self-defense or martial arts courses. You can find these locally. But, if you have no local options or would rather do the training on your own time online, again consider The "Self Defense Company" (myselfdefensetraining.com). Note that we suggest using force *only* as self-defense, and *only* after all other options have been used.

Third, being manly is typically a matter of your interests. Whether you like it or not, being a fan of "My Little Pony" doesn't make you manly. No woman will say she wants to date a guy like that and putting "Brony" on your resume will pretty much keep you working at McDonald's. It's not just this extreme example that holds true. Any guy whose interests are more on the feminine side, as defined by current trends, will find himself at a disadvantage with women. Some examples of girly interests are female-oriented media (Twilight, Dave Matthews Band), typically feminine pursuits (fashion, hair and nail design, sharing recipes on Pinterest), etc.

You might be objecting that your girly interest is a core part of your personality. If so, maybe your datelessness has less to do with your height than you previously assumed. For example, I know a perpetually dateless guy who is always talking about his man "time of the month" and his love for "chick flicks" on Facebook. He is almost always single and he's over six foot!

So, you need to go out and pursue some manly interests. Here are a few examples: sports and athletics (playing and watching), cars (appreciating and repairing), home repairs/upkeep, grilling, carpentry, shooting/hunting, boxing, etc. Also, I'd add a few others to the list: the hard sciences and even traditional artistic endeavors like writing, painting, and photography. You don't get much manlier than guys like Picasso and Hemingway.

Notice how these interests are all related to providing and protecting in some way? Sports show that you are tough (or at least appreciate toughness), while the others should be pretty obvious in their connection to providing for or protecting a woman. Even artistic endeavors show intelligence and creativity, both traits that prove you can more than take care of yourself in a world of dummies.

You might think I'm encouraging guys to be macho assholes. I'm not. Even with the above examples, you need to keep it masculine, not macho. Most macho guys aren't confident or manly; they are insecure types who desperately want you to *think* they are manly, and try too hard doing it. You never want to turn into a stereotype. For example, you can legally and responsibly shoot a gun. That's manly. Discharging a weapon recklessly is just idiotic (and illegal).

I'm not asking you to give up your other interests, except maybe the creepy ones. You can still collect records, have a love for stamps, or whatever else. But, you'll need to add some manly interests to that as well, at least if you want to date attractive women. While it's possible to luck into dates without being masculine, you're not going to do it very often. Oh, and yes, a man liking "My Little Pony" is creepy.

Fourth, masculinity is often a function of testosterone levels. Numerous studies have shown that men with higher levels of testosterone are more successful both in business and with women. And, don't think that tall guys naturally have more testosterone. It's not always the case. But, it doesn't matter anyway because it's possible to raise your testosterone.

Also, let me just add that science has shown that testosterone isn't linked to anger or rage or anything like that. Its presence is actually correlated with being calm, logical, relaxed, and confident. In other words, elevated testosterone is connected to high-value male traits. Those overgrown children who pick fights and go into rages aren't filled with testosterone. They just have anger problems. Or maybe they're taking steroids. But, whatever the source, it's not testosterone.

A quick and easy way to boost testosterone is to get out there and exercise. Yes, that actually raises a guy's testosterone. Perhaps that's one reason why so many guys today play video games all day at home while remaining dateless: because they're lazy and overweight. If that's you, get off your butt and start working out! Not only will you look better and be more high-value, but you'll boost that testosterone too.

While all types of exercise can help, the two best for boosting your testosterone are weight lifting and interval training. Both do different things to your body, so you might need to choose one or the other. Lifting weights will increase your bulk. Lots of short guys, myself included, don't like the stocky look. If so, go for the intense interval training (like Beachbody's "Insanity" or "P90x"). Those, or similar programs, will give you a lean, fit look and send the testosterone through the roof.

Also, did you know that manly activities can raise your testosterone levels? Studies have shown that after chopping wood a man's testosterone goes up. Pretty cool huh? So, pursue some of those masculine hobbies that I mentioned earlier and you'll get the added benefit of a testosterone boost.

Diet also plays a role in testosterone levels. Believe it or not, higher fat diets tend to increase testosterone. That doesn't mean you need to go out and start eating cake. It does mean that you'll want to increase your testosterone by raising your consumption of healthy meats, eggs, nuts, etc.

You'll also want to cut out the junk food. Empty carbs and sugars take up valuable calorie intake that you could put towards testosterone raising foods (and refined carbs make you fat).

Another way some guys attempt to boost testosterone is through taking supplements. However, I don't really advise this because a lot of the alleged testosterone boosting supplements don't work and they can have bad side effects. Nonetheless, I've seen some promising research related to the herb Fenugreek. I've also had some personal success with it. Since it's used in cooking and has been for a long time, it also appears to be pretty safe. However, consult a doctor and proceed carefully with any type of supplementation.

Finally, I want to discuss body language. It is a major way to make you look more like a man. It's especially important for short guys because we need to project more confidence with our bodies because they're naturally smaller and less imposing.

Chapter 20 is devoted to body language, and deals with this topic in more detail. Read that and look at the confidence poses. They will go a long way in helping you appear more masculine. In addition, some of the poses even raise your testosterone. Yes, sitting or standing a certain way has been shown to change your body's chemistry.

Your homework for this chapter is to evaluate your level of manliness and, if it's not high enough, then fix it. Have you started to be more high-value? Do you have an attitude of manliness? Are your interests that of a real man? Do you think you are filled with testosterone or are you more of a "manboob" type of guy?

Evaluate where you stand and list action steps to become manlier. Use the ideas in this chapter and come up with more of your own. As a short guy, it's extremely important that you don't appear childlike or girly because that's the first assumption many people have due to your lack of stature. Let them know, from the second they meet you, you're just as much a man as anyone else in the room (if not more of a man).

CHAPTER NINE

COOL AND DETACHED

When I was a teacher, I had students who simply freaked out when it came time to take a test. I could tell from class discussion that they knew the material and were smart, but they were so convinced of the need for success on a test that it literally crippled their ability to...you guessed it...take the test!

On the other hand, the students who were more relaxed about the test usually did better (or at least performed according to their level of preparation). Those who were anxious about tests never performed to their (usually insane) level of preparation.

My students who performed poorly on tests are a great example of attachment, which is when we are overly focused on and anxious about an outcome. The opposite of attachment is detachment (sometimes the word "non-attachment" is used). Detachment is doing the next best thing without worrying about or anticipating a particular outcome. It is sometimes referred to as acting in an "outcome independent" way, because you do what is right without worrying about the outcome. Being attached creates all sorts of anxiety and pressure, while detachment allows a person to be relaxed, calm, and excellent.

Detachment is a very tough concept for many people to achieve (and that's even for those making an effort to detach). So, don't be surprised if you're a very attached individual. By default, most of us are. Even though true detachment is a sign of advanced spiritual enlightenment in Eastern religions, don't think you're getting out of learning how to do it.

In my experience, shorter guys are some of the most attached people on this planet, especially in regards to dating. Here's why. Taller guys, with their natural advantages in getting a date, can often luck their way into at least a few relationships, even without dating skills. So, many of them aren't desperate for women. And, especially when they're young, they get their egos built up by peers and adults, hearing how talented and amazing they are, even when they're not.

Short men, on the other hand, tend to get beaten down by their classmates and authority figures. And, they're rarely praised as much as taller boys. The circumstances of life tend to make shorter guys at least a little (or a lot) more desperate. Any normal man who goes months or even years (or a lifetime) without so much as basic romantic attention from a woman will start to get desperate and even bitter.

However, a desperate guy is never, ever attractive. Yet, when our biology makes us desperate for women, it's really difficult to fight it. So, short guys, who already have a disadvantage, typically add desperation to the mix, meaning they come across as an angry or whiny stereotype. While short men need to overcome that attitude and stop being so desperate, such a feeling is perfectly normal.

Now, however, it's time to get over it. Just like with the venting chapter, we're going to acknowledge it and move on. But, it's going to mean making an effort to curb those feelings of desperation and attachment, or at least stop showing them to others. Just like the smart kids who couldn't take tests, if you know the skills to land a date, but are desperately attached to the idea of getting a date, then you'll still fail.

Your main goal is to stop caring so much about women. Short guys tend to fetishize having a girlfriend because many of them don't get one very often. This leads to a couple of things. First, they tend to put women on a pedestal, thinking that women are the greatest thing in the world. Second, when they don't receive the object of their desires, they get angry and bitter, ready to dismiss the entire sex from their lives (and maybe the planet).

So, your first goal of becoming more detached is to put women in the right perspective. Women are human beings, just like you. Yes, even the pretty ones. Women are not better, more pure, more noble, smarter, nicer, or anything else. Each woman has her good and bad points, as well as accomplishments and failures. Women, like men, can be total losers, and jerks.

You must be realistic and calm about the female sex if you want any success. Take them down from the pedestal when you're happy and pull them up from the pit when you're mad. Keep an even keel about the ladies. They are just people and, above all, you have the ability (or are learning it through this book) to date them.

Second, you might have trouble with detachment because you're anxious and uptight. That's often more of a personality trait than a short guy thing, but I still know a ton of short guys who are anxious. It probably comes from some of the issues shorter men face. However, anxiety and uptightness aren't attractive to women (or anyone).

You'll have to learn to relax. I recommend meditating regularly. Meditation can help you center yourself and achieve an underlying sense of relaxation, even in the midst of stress. A great book on meditation is Mindfulness For Beginners and Wherever You Go, There You Are, both by Jon Kabat-Zinn.

Take five minutes or more each day for yourself. Use it to pray, meditate, or relax. If it helps, you can create a more traditional meditation space (candles, etc.). What matters is that you are alone and not distracted. Your goal during this time is be mindful of the present. Kabat-Zinn, mentioned above, defines being mindful as "paying attention on purpose non-judgmentally in the present moment as if your life depended on it." In other words, just be aware of the present, removing all thoughts of women, work, bills, and any other stress that isn't present with you at that instant.

Sometimes meditation can be challenging. When a thought enters your head that isn't related to the present moment (like negative self-talk or thoughts of that girl from work), just refocus back to the present.

Third, you'll have to learn to relax and be cool. Being cool is a high-value trait. Think of how it's entered our language. Calling someone "cool" is a great compliment, like the cool boss or the cool teacher. It's one of the highest compliments a person can be paid from a social perspective.

Being cool is not just being relaxed, but remaining calm in high-stress situations. Some of the greatest fighters and warriors are cool because they remain calm and poised while everyone else freaks out. Every time life throws you a curve ball, take a few deep breaths and keep calm. Don't overreact. If you can be the coolest guy in the room, you'll have a huge advantage in both business and dating. Being cool may be easier said than done, but if you meditate regularly, you will start to find yourself becoming calmer and stronger in any situation, even stressful ones.

Finally, true detachment, especially with women, is the result of having options. Realize that there are many ways to achieve your dating goals. It's not only liberating to know that there are many paths to a chosen goal, but it can even be fun to experience the pleasant surprises that arise when we are on the way to realizing our dreams. This book is going to expand your map of the world by giving you many, many options!

Having options also means you have a variety of women at your disposal, and you are not focused on one particular girl or "crush." This is easier said than done, especially at this point in your life. But, ultimately, you want to have so many women at your disposal that losing out on one simply doesn't matter.

Let me say a few things about what detachment isn't. Detachment isn't aimlessness. A person must set goals if he wants to be successful. However, detachment means having a relaxed, non-anxious attitude towards achieving those goals. If you never set goals, you'll be detached for sure, but you'll also be single and likely doing very little in life.

Detachment also isn't about being lazy. Lazy people just don't pursue any goals, even if they have set them. Sitting on your couch isn't detachment; it just means you're too lazy to get off your butt. You must have passion and dedication if you want any type of personal change and this includes developing the skills to meet women.

In the definition I provided earlier, I mentioned that detachment involves doing the next best thing. In other words, you should always be excellent and striving for more excellence. But, by being detached, you're being excellent because that's who you are, so you're relaxed about the outcome. That gives you the freedom and flexibility to always make the best decisions. Far from creating lazy stoners, embracing detachment means you're more likely to reach your goals and properly direct your hard work.

Your assignment is to start (or continue) a regular practice of meditation. Take a few minutes out of every day to center yourself and work on mindfulness and detachment. Go somewhere you can be alone and relaxed, cater the setting to your personal tastes (candles, etc.), and just start by taking deep breaths.

Become aware of your breathing and mindfully focus on your breaths. Be aware of the sights and smells, and savor the present moment. If you find your mind wandering to that girl who put you down three weeks ago, return your attention to your breathing. Relax and let past issues and future worries disappear. Live in the present throughout your meditation.

Try to increase your meditation time as you move forward. But, even if you can't, make an effort to be more mindful and relaxed in your everyday life. Resist the urge to flip out or be stressed. Think of the relaxation of your meditation times and apply that to all your stressful situations. If in doubt, no matter where you are, just start breathing more slowly and pay attention to your breaths. It will really help with your relaxation.

Chapter Ten

Assert Yourself

Back in graduate school, my brother and I were asked to handle part of the financial duties at a church we attended. We hated math and knew nothing about accounting. As they took us through the process of depositing and cataloging the money, we were completely lost. We both wanted to say "no" badly. But, you can probably guess what happened. We agreed and it was a disaster. Fortunately, no money was lost or mismanaged. But, the stress on us was crazy.

I was a classic "yes man." I would say "yes" to just about every request. Check that. Every request. I was constantly getting roped into doing things that I didn't want to do or couldn't do. At one teaching job, I got roped into doing just about every activity imaginable. My payment for being so agreeable for five years? I was laid off. What a great reward!

I had let myself become the guy everyone turned to when they needed someone to help them, whether legitimately or selfishly. I let people walk all over me and rarely stood up for my beliefs and interests. It really sucked because I didn't want to be subservient to the needs of others all the time. I wanted to stand up for myself; I just didn't have the courage.

Many guys, of all heights, are just like me. However, from my experience, short guys suffer from this problem more so than taller men. Being smaller, we are less naturally intimidating. So, instead of losing fights, we just avoid them by saying "yes" at the start.

Being assertive is a high-value trait, for a couple of reasons. It proves that a guy can provide and protect because he's confident and powerful enough to stand up for himself. Assertiveness is also a pretty rare trait. Among guys, you'll find aggression, on one hand, and passivity on the other. But, a truly assertive person doesn't come along every day.

Let's look at the wrong ways to behave first. They aren't attractive (although, of all the "wrong" choices, aggression is probably the most attractive to women) and they're usually ineffective at getting one's own way in the long run.

Aggression: Using physical, emotional, or another type of force to achieve one's way. Can be effective short term, but long term it is rarely effective.

Passivity: Dealing with issues by ignoring them; "going with the flow." Rarely effective to achieve success. Only "works" in the sense that any confrontation may be delayed. It is a survival mechanism in that it gets the person ignored, kind of like when an animal hides or "freezes."

Passive-Aggression: Hiding aggressive intent (barely) under a passive response. This is expressed as being nice (passive) to someone's face, while planning (or threatening) aggressive acts behind the person's back.

Let's look at a scenario and see the different responses at work.

A single girl you have a crush on is eating with you at the lunch table at work. Some guy makes a comment about shorter guys and she says, "I'd never date shorties. They're not all man…total manlets."

Clearly, such a statement is hurtful and demands a response. Here are the three wrong ways to respond.

Aggressiveness: "You are such a dumb bitch."

Passivity: [silence]

Passive-Aggression: (five minutes later to your male buddy) "That girl from accounting is such a bitch. I think I'm going to tell the boss that I saw her come into work late three days last month."

Obviously, the first one is highly inappropriate in a work setting. Passivity isn't the best option because I doubt any short man really wants to remain silent. He wants to respond and stand up for himself, but likely doesn't have the courage to do it. The passive-aggressive response just makes a guy look weak and petty. And, he knows he hasn't really addressed the issue, so that response won't even make him feel better! What this scenario needs is an assertive response.

A good, assertive response would be something like: "I think that's a really ignorant comment. You might not want to date short guys, which is fine. But, I can assure you, there are short men who are far manlier than you can even imagine."

Being more assertive will definitely make you appear like a provider and protector and thus make you more attractive to women. In addition, it will give you the courage to speak your mind to them and others in your life who might try to dominate you, put you down, or take advantage of you. Our advice to be assertive is this:

Just say it: If you have something to say and it's appropriate, express it, even if others will disagree or it might be controversial. Don't hold back and forever think of what you could've said.

Stand up for yourself: You should never, ever let yourself get bad-mouthed or intimidated. Now, there are times when it might be best to be silent or even get the hell out of there (like when you're a victim of crime). But, in most cases, you must assert your position or rights.

Speak clearly and with a deep voice: If you want to be taken seriously, your tone of voice and pitch are very important. Shorter guys sometimes have higher voices, which stops them from being considered credible. If you know you're going to have to stand up and assert yourself, then purposefully lower your voice and speak slowly and clearly.

Use decisive wording: A lot of guys hedge on their language because they're afraid of offending someone. In college and graduate school, the powers-that-be tell us to write in a way that doesn't offend anybody, so many of us have gotten used to hedging everything we say to the point that what comes out of our mouths is pure pabulum.

Examples of hedge words are "think," "might," "seems," etc. So, if you're going to decisively talk to someone, don't hedge your words. For example, don't say, "It seems there's a problem and I think I need to talk to you about it." Instead, be clear and consistent. Say, "There's a problem and I need to talk to you about it."

Never apologize when you didn't do anything: Many passive guys make the mistake of apologizing even when they are not at fault. For example, a co-worker runs into you. Instead of apologizing for her mistake, say something funny, or let her apologize and then assure her it is all good. If you have a legitimate request, never preface it with "I'm sorry." Many teachers will say, "I'm sorry, but you can't do that." Instead, be firm and clear, and quit apologizing for doing what is right or neutral.

Be calm: When being assertive, avoid acting too passionate, either one way or another. Passion can be good, but not when trying to be assertive. If you're whiny, emotional, or even angry, you'll lose the power that comes from assertiveness. This is especially true of short people because society doesn't expect them to remain cool and calm. Society does, however, expect them to be angry and whiny.

Be respectful: The purpose of asserting yourself is to be heard and possibly get something you want. Don't go out of your way to be a jerk without necessary cause. If you can show respect to the other person while still demonstrating your power, you'll likely get respect back, even if it's grudging.

Also, it's worth mentioning that, in most cases, being assertive is not going to lose you friends. It is an admired trait so it could actually win you more friends and lovers. However, there might be times where your assertiveness could be controversial.

In that case, roll with it. Don't be passive just because a few people might be offended. All of the great leaders and role models in the world have offended a good number of people. We don't study the passive and nice guys in the history books, nor has there ever been a passive movie hero.

For practice, I'd like you to list situations where you need to assert yourself. It could be to stand up to a bullying co-worker or to go ask your brother-in-law for the money back that you lent him two years ago. Whatever it is, list it. Then, outline how you can assert yourself with the person in question using the tips above.

I reached a point in my life where I realized that going with the flow and being a passive guy got me nowhere. Once I was let go from my job, I finally woke up and started to assert myself. If I was going to lose out in the future, at least I would do so knowing that I said what needed to be said and stood up for myself.

Chapter Eleven

Be Funny

When my friends and I go out, whether it's to a restaurant, club, or any social function, we unleash our humor on the place. And, because we are naturally funny, have great material, and think on our feet, we become the center of attention very quickly. It gets to the point where sometimes everyone is crowding around us because no one is sure what we're going to even say next (sometimes we aren't even sure)!

Many studies have shown that women consider funny guys to be very attractive. Scientists speculate that humor demonstrates a man's high-value by showing that he is intelligent and clever. A guy who can be genuinely funny telegraphs to women that he is smart enough to be a powerful provider and protector.

Studies also demonstrate that women find "humor generators" attractive while men prefer "humor appreciators." In other words, women like men who are funny and men like women who find them funny (see: psychologytoday.com/articles/200508/humors-sexual-side).

Legitimately funny men are pretty rare, which is another reason why humor is such a highly valued trait. While anyone can slap together a few fecal jokes or repeat something from the internet, real humor is a bit of art form. Obviously, your humor has to be pretty good if you're going to show a girl that you are intelligent. This chapter is going to explain the different types of humor and offer some basic advice on executing routines.

I should add that laughter has been shown, through various scientific studies, to have many health benefits. It lowers stress, increases immune system response, and decreases blood pressure. Laughing also releases endorphins, the hormones that make people happy. In addition, it's hard to be angry, resentful, fearful, or generally negative while laughing. Humor gives us a good feeling and that's what most of us really want!

In spite of the obvious benefits of laughter, most people, especially adults, don't get nearly enough of it. However, from my experience, I don't think most people want such little humor in their lives. It's just the way we've been conditioned to think through years of humorless institutions that have told us over and over again not to laugh.

However, one of the reasons that more adults don't laugh is that most people simply aren't funny. And when unfunny people try to be funny, it's often painful and awkward.

Two things make humor effective on an evolutionary level. The first is incongruity. If something is incongruent, it "doesn't fit." This could be anything from a joke that has no punch line to a picture of a dog wearing glasses or an uptight, nicely dressed man doing something out of character.

It sounds kind of abstract at first, but you can use incongruity to great effect in your daily interactions. It's one of my favorite ways to make people laugh. For example, I use a tip I learned from Joshua Wagner and inject (pardon the pun) drug related humor into the conversation. I'll order a coffee with cream, sweetener, and meth.

Most people do a double-take, then break into laughter. It's very incongruent because, first of all, it's not a typical coffee order. The incongruity is increased by the fact that I have a fit body, clear skin, and great teeth. If I were an obvious methamphetamine junkie, then such a coffee order would be congruent and an occasion for sadness or revulsion, not humor.

The second aspect of successful humor is creating some hypothetical discomfort while everyone is in a position of safety. This explains why people find troubling things, like getting kicked in the balls, funny only when they are not actually experiencing the troubling thing. Humor originally may have functioned as a way for humans to relax after a stressful event. Once the danger had passed (say from a battle or hunting trip), the men of the tribe would laugh about the situation as a way to relieve the stress.

This is why we find other people getting scared funny, but only from the comfort of our living rooms. If the situation were real (or it was happening to us), it wouldn't be funny at all. Even if it were a joke, in the moment, it would still be scary and we couldn't laugh until we settled down and realized it was a joke. It is why a guy asking for meth in his coffee in a safe restaurant is funny, but not so funny if you are taking care of your meth-addicted brother or getting accosted by a homeless junkie on the street.

When using humor in public, you must always keep safety in mind. This doesn't mean that since a girl looks to be in a safe situation, you can unleash any type of humor. Simply put, jokes about race, violence, and sex will take away the feeling of safety for many people because these topics have caused them pain in the past (or could). This is why I rarely joke about drugs if I can tell the person I am speaking to has used them, or if I know a relative of theirs has.

Another important way to be funny is to use situational or observational humor. This is adapting your jokes to whatever is happening at that moment. For example, if you are sitting in a crowded restaurant, situational humor would find ways to be funny based around what you encounter at your table or the bar.

This type of humor is beneficial because it has to be original and it makes you look intelligent and quick on your feet, both high-value traits. Situational humor can also be based around current events. Once again, using information found in the news or popular culture proves that you pay attention and are intelligent.

Two other types of humor you may want to consider using are anti-humor and the shaggy dog story. They are very similar and I have found both of these very effective in my years of winning over men and women.

Anti-humor is telling a story or a joke that is so purposefully unfunny that it elicits laughter from the person listening. The earlier example of putting meth in coffee is anti-humor at work. Meth abuse is not a traditionally funny topic (for good reason). Sometimes when my friends and I first use the "joke," the employees will give us a bewildered look. However, once they realize we are kidding (and not real meth users), they start to laugh. However, notice there is no real joke or punch line. Another example of anti-humor is saying, "Did you hear the joke about the alcoholic? Yeah, he got liver disease and died." It is totally not funny in a traditional sense, but elicits laughter as anti-humor.

A shaggy dog story is a long, pointless story, usually with ridiculous details and an absurd conclusion. These can be especially effective if delivered with a straight face. For example, once when David and I were at a water park, we were telling a girl about how before I lost a bunch of weight I got stuck in one of the slides and they had to use the jaws of life to get me out. And, I celebrated my rescue with a giant ham dinner.

Remember that shaggy dog stories work best with incongruity, so you must make sure that if you're telling an alleged story about yourself that it is incongruent with your personality or other traits. In my example, I was shirtless at a water park, so she could tell I was in great shape. The story was totally BS and everyone knew it. But, for my listeners, it was like being sucked into a brief, funny fantasy.

Just remember when trying to be humorous that doing something for shock value is rarely funny. In addition, humor is one area where it's possible to be very creepy. Telling jokes about inappropriate topics can make others extremely uncomfortable, especially if you generally look and act like a weirdo.

Finally, use your judgment to determine when and how to be funny. I knew a guy who actually walked into a funeral and started doing his shtick. Needless to say, they tossed him out of the church (quite literally) and he lost several friends. Make sure you read every situation before throwing out your humor.

I want to include a few words about creating humor routines so that you can have some funny material up your sleeve in social situations. To make yourself look the highest-value, you should have a large repertoire of funny stories, lines, and other material that you can effortlessly whip out without much thought at a moment's notice.

From a comedy standpoint, a routine is just a series of funny stories, lines, jokes, etc. They are not one-off comments or jokes, but sustained attempts at being funny for a longer period of time. The best comedian's routines will effortlessly shift from theme to theme and "stack" jokes, lines, and stories so that the audience remains captivated hypnotically for the entire show. When you go out and meet new people, you'll want to have enough routines to keep people laughing and enjoying your presence for as long as you're with them.

When making routines, you have three options: make your own, find someone else's, or create a mixture of the two. I would advise that in the beginning you pick option three and eventually move on to just making your own. I would never recommend using someone else's routines unchanged. They can be very unnatural because they don't reflect your life situation. Not only that, if you're simply using memorized material, it will seem too "canned," kind of like using pick-up lines. And people hate pick-up lines because the only skill they require is memorizing something you read on the internet.

My advice is to first find some general humor routines on the internet, but you can also search for websites that specialize in creating funny material. Then, practice doing the routines, adapting them to your personality and your interests. It's key that if you use other people's material as a base that you make it your own.

Second, you'll have to actually practice the routines. I recommend that you practice with family and friends first. You'll find out what works and what doesn't in a low-pressure environment. View it like a lab. If a routine doesn't work, then you may have to junk it. If parts of it don't work, then you'll know what to get rid of before going "live."

After some practicing and adapting, the routine should become natural. If your routines don't flow and aren't authentic, then you'll come across as a bad amateur stand-up comedian. It's better to use moderately funny original material than to have proven routines fail because you can't deliver them authentically. This is also why practice in low-pressure environments is important.

A high-value guy is always crafting, learning, and perfecting new routines. Your routines should also be adaptable to every situation. In many cases, it's just a matter of shifting a few details or mentally picking the right routine at the right time. This is important to remember because situational humor is more personal, which means you'll get the best laughs and be the most memorable to a girl.

Also, routines should never be a crutch to avoid coming up with original material on the fly. This becomes easier the more you practice and as you consciously work to craft new routines and modify your existing ones.

If you are stuck and can't think of a topic for original routines, try to recall funny stories or memorable events from your life. Then adapt them to specific situations. Perhaps you can use a routine about getting lost when you went camping when you were twelve. Maybe you can base one around an interesting story you heard from someone else. Just make sure your content is funny, authentic, and adaptable.

Keep in mind when writing routines that the stories about yourself should never make you look low-value or creepy. If your routines involve some personal foible or funny incident, make sure they are cute and lighthearted. Funny personal stories should always reinforce your positive traits or at least be neutral. They should never bring down your value in anyone's eyes.

Is it okay to poke fun of your height in your routines? I would say "yes" if you are really confident. If not, pointing out how short you are, and poking fun at it, might qualify as bringing down your value. Self-deprecating humor is hard to pull off, so early on you might want to avoid it. But, if you're feeling really brave, then go for it.

For your practice assignment, I'd like you to watch a few hours of great comedians. You can also read funny articles or stories. Cracked.com has some excellent material. These should give you an idea of how humor works and how to tell stories, deliver punch-lines, etc. If you know a funny person, then go out and watch him in action. Yes, watch a man. Women have a different sense of humor. Take mental notes and see how he elicits laughter.

To complete this chapter, write out at least two routines and practice them. I want these to be completely original! Make sure to throw in plenty of incongruity and observational humor, but don't violate the rule of safety. Include a short shaggy dog story or an example of anti-humor into one of them. The point is to practice writing routines, not to write stand up worthy material right now.

Next chance you get, I want you to practice what you've just written with someone you trust. These are your stories, so they should be natural and authentic. However, in high-stress environments like meeting strangers you may not be able to deliver your routines with ease. So, have your friend or family member give you feedback, not only on the material itself, but also on your delivery, timing, and so on. Humor will probably be the most important weapon you have to influence and win over others.

However, let me add one point about humor. Your goal when interacting with women isn't just to entertain them, but to get them to date you. You'll want to get them laughing and feeling good, for sure. However, make sure the conversation is a mix of lighthearted banter and more serious topics (including sexual escalation). You don't want to be perceived as only a figure of fun or an entertainer.

Chapter Twelve

The Art Of Teasing

When David and I order food, we will often use a particular routine on the female employees. We essentially rate their service. We will make a comment like, "You're doing a very good job today. I think I'd rate you a…B-." We do it with smiles on our faces and in an obviously flirtatious type of way.

Without exception, the employees pretend to be indignant and ask us why we'd give them such a low grade. We make a few other jokes and then continue to talk with them. However, this little routine works like a charm because we get a lot more attention from them. Not only do they take an interest in us socially, but they become more eager to please us as customers as well.

This is sometimes called "negging" in the pick-up artist communities, but it's actually just playful teasing. We've separated this chapter from the humor section because it's a somewhat different skillset than being funny. But, it's related because men who are funny are also some of the best at teasing women.

Teasing girls is effective at making them like you for a couple of reasons. First, they typically love it because you're giving them attention. If you think about it, you are paying attention to them, just in a backhanded sort of way. Lots of people today have grown up without adequate male attention. As unfortunate as this is, it means that many women are starved for a man's attention and will positively respond, even to light teasing. And, women know that it's flirting (if you do it correctly) and all but the most uptight ones will enjoy it.

Second, teasing gives their self-esteem a little hit. Teasing is good natured, but it's nonetheless a put down. Teasing often gets the girl wondering if what you said is really true and thinking about what she can do to get you to like her. This is why teasing is very effective with prettier women. They're used to getting compliments (usually from passive guys they would never date), not teased. When you tease them, it creates anxiety that maybe they're not "all that" after all.

If the idea of teasing a girl seems bad, then you still need to knock women off the pedestal in your mind. This is the dating game. Lots of these beautiful women have absolutely savaged guys whom they didn't like (maybe one was you). Throwing out some lighthearted teasing that makes their already giant ego a little less huge isn't doing any lasting damage. If you want to win the dating game (i.e. get a relationship), you'll have to gain the upper hand.

Third, teasing shows you are confident and dominant. You are showing your confidence by leading the conversation in a flirtatious way, thus taking a bold social risk. Teasing also shows that you are edgy and assertive, and distinguishes you from typical males who fall over themselves to spew sycophantic drivel at women. Thus, teasing is a great way to avoid being "friend-zoned."

So, it's okay to tease women. You're not being mean or offensive. You're joking with them. If you get to the point where you're angry and putting them down, you've turned into a creepy jerk. That's not teasing and it's not attractive. Lots of guys try to tease and it turns into this. Don't make that mistake.

The key to teasing effectively is to always keep your underlying attitude light and relaxed. Operate with the goal of having fun and flirting; never tease from anger or resentment. Be detached when you tease women. If you let years of rejection guide your teasing, I promise you that you'll cross the line into angry and creepy. If the girl has truly pissed you off, then don't even try to tease. Just walk away.

Also, when teasing, you'll have to pay special attention to both her and her environment. Like general humor, the best teasing is always observational. Your jabs must be specific to that woman. Teasing a girl about a trait that all girls share won't get you anywhere. What if she bucks the stereotype? Then, you look like an idiot.

Look for unique traits. Maybe it's her hair, way of dressing, or unusual shoes. Draw attention to that when you tease her. Remember, this shows that you are paying attention to her, even if it's in a non-traditional way.

Here are examples of good teasing:

"I really like your hair."
(Girl says, "Thanks").
"You're welcome. Not every girl can rock the 'I just got out of bed' look, but it looks great on you."

"You're doing a great job with my meal. Don't worry I always tip a certain percent for waitresses like you."
(Girl says, "That's sweet").
"Did you know 'zero' is a percent?"

You can see how the process works. Always smile and be jovial when you say stuff like this, and when dealing with a waitress, to be cool, make sure you quickly tell her you are just joking. Notice how in both examples above, the girl is getting a compliment…of sorts. But, then again, not really. The best teases catch a girl off guard because women are used to receiving compliments. Teasing flips the script. It essentially puts you, the man, squarely in charge of the interaction.

We've included eleven free teases in "Appendix A" because we want to get you started (and give you some good material). However, the best teases are always ones you think of on the fly and that you tailor to specific girls and specific situations. You won't appear terribly high-value if you're only using our material, especially when it's not appropriate.

For your assignment, read our teases and write a few more that you think would be useful in most environments (or even specific ones). It's good to always have a repertoire of at least ten to fifteen teases that you can draw from, even if you adapt them to specific circumstances (which, of course, you should).

Next, go out and practice teasing girls. Believe it or not, it's effective with girls of all ages. Tease five year olds and ninety year olds and everyone in between. Obviously with the young ones (and probably the old ones), you don't want any sexual edge. But, females of all ages love being teased just so it doesn't turn into meanness.

When you go out and practice teasing, observe how it is often (especially if you intend it to be) taken as flirting. I hope this helps you realize that women love being teased. And, that it's an effective way to make you look both high-value and funny.

Before I end this chapter, I need to mention a few caveats about teasing. First, don't tease high-value guys unless they're your friends and it's an expected part of the relationship. For example, David and I tease our buddies (and they tease back). If that type of relationship hasn't been established yet, teasing a guy is a good way to get yourself punched (or if it's a boss, lose your job). And it may build resentment in guys that are less confident than you.

Second, some girls have such low self-esteem that they fail to catch that your teasing is flirting. For example, many women whom you consider pretty may hate their looks. If you flirt with these girls about their hair or another physical attribute, they may get offended. I have found that women who rarely get male attention are often very suspicious of attention when they do get it. If you find this is the case, you may have to confidently "save face" by saying something like, "Hey, you know I was just kidding right? I actually like your hair." Remember, you are teasing to get her to *like* you, not hate you!

Third, avoid teasing in inappropriate environments, especially professional ones. Some women separate work and play quite sharply and will not welcome any kind of teasing at work, even if they would absolutely flirt back if you had said it at a club on Saturday night.

CHAPTER THIRTEEN

PHYSICAL LOOKS

A few months ago, my brother and I were giving a talk and met a beautiful young lady who was a big fan of our work. She approached and started talking to us. When she told us that she was twenty-six, we told her how young she was. She looked puzzled and said, "You can't be that much older than I am, can you?" She couldn't believe we had nine years on her.

We both get this kind of feedback all the time. We have great bodies. We look seven or eight years younger than our actual ages. We have nice hair. Our eyes are "lady killers" (or so we've been told). I could go on and on. I'm very proud of the fact that, although I'm a thirty-six year old short guy, I'm still very good looking. I'm proud because I've worked damn hard for nearly every one of my physical attributes. Okay, admittedly the eyes were a genetic gift, but I use them correctly.

We could go on and on, but we'd rather focus on helping you hear those same compliments because you work to look the absolute best you can.

Although looks aren't the primary way to push a woman's attraction buttons, they still are highly valued. So, you definitely benefit by having good looks. This includes being fit and handsome, as well as what you put on your body. We are still a very physical appearance oriented society. Plus, as a short man, you already have a deficit in the eyes of most people (your height). It's imperative that you make up for that in other ways.

My advice to short men regarding their looks is to do everything (as much as is possible) right. You can't change your height, so you have to make sure all other aspects of your physical appearance are top-notch. With that in mind, I'm going to address a few areas and give tips on how to look your absolute best. I'll start with the top and work my way down. I will address weight and fitness in a separate chapter.

Hair

It's best if you have some and that it's a contemporary style. But, have a haircut that's contemporary *for your age*. In other words, don't look like you're forty trying to appear fifteen. If you're balding, then you have options. Minoxidil (Rogaine) and Propecia both help you keep the hair you already have and (possibly) re-grow some of it. Minoxidil is extremely cheap (about ten dollars for a month's supply) and is available in the United States over-the-counter.

If you're already bald, then your only options are a hair transplant or toupee. Both aren't really great choices, but you can consider them. The best choice for balding guys is to probably just shave your entire head. That's the most masculine of options. Definitely don't do a comb-over or let your hair on the sides grow super long. It doesn't look manly.

Face

The face is a major area where guys are judged on their looks. A lot of your facial looks are beyond your control outside of plastic surgery. However, you can help yourself look your best.

Keep your face clean and moisturized. This goes a long way towards avoiding the haggard look or appearing older than you are. Speaking of that, if you are looking a little on the old side, try something like Retin-A (tretinoin), an FDA approved cream that can reduce fine lines and wrinkles. Your best bet to avoid looking too old is to avoid a lot of sun exposure. Use sunblock when you're outside, even during the winter.

As far as facial hair goes, lots of short guys fear the boyish look, so they trade it for the fugly look by growing beards. You can keep a little stubble if you fear looking too much like a baby face. But, avoid the long beards. Your friends may think you look cool, but, and this is the honest truth, I rarely see bearded guys with beautiful women. They're mostly dudes in "bromances "with other guys.

Keep the nose hair, eyebrows, and ear hair trimmed. You might not notice the hair growing there, but women do. It may seem like a pain, but remember, you need to do everything right. You can buy three-in-one trimmers that will easily and painlessly take care of these areas.

Chest/Waist/Legs And Below

The major issue here for grooming is general hygiene because this is inclusive of the body's smelliest parts. You'll definitely want to keep your entire body washed. This means showering at least daily and always after workouts or sweating a lot. You'll want to make especially sure that your underarms, crotch, and butt area are clean. They can really stink.

Always use deodorant under the arms and reapply if necessary throughout the day. Cologne is a plus too. Choose a masculine scent (I use Cool Water, Curve, and Inner Realm) and use a couple of sprays. Don't overdo it or you'll make people choke. That's not very attractive. I often keep cologne and deodorant in my briefcase.

The only other issue surrounding these body parts is hair. Should you remove body hair or not? I generally recommend not having chest and back hair, especially if you look like a Silverback Gorilla from a distance. If you have a nice body, going hairless accentuates that and makes it more visible. Any hair-related questions below the belt are up to you. I'm definitely not going to go there. But, I have to add that I don't recommend shaving your legs because it's girly.

You have a few options for unwanted hair: laser removal, waxing, sugaring, or shaving. I've listed them in the order of permanence. Laser removal is good because it's permanent, but bad because it's costly. Waxing and sugaring rip out hair, and cause it to take a while to grow back. Plus, you can do them at home and they're cheap. But, they are extremely painful, especially the first time, and can be messy. Shaving is the easiest and cheapest option. But, your hair will start to grow back in about two to three days.

Feet/Hands

The feet are another area that you should wash thoroughly and regularly. Stinky feet are a huge turn-off. The smell is just nasty. In addition, wash your socks after wearing them for the day.

Change shoes when they start to smell, or preferably have multiple pairs that you can wear on alternate days. If you have to, put odor absorbers in your shoes.

As far as hands go, keep your hands nice and moisturized. Crusty hands are gross. In addition, trim your fingernails properly. Once again, women notice these things. Biting your nails looks very unattractive.

Clothing

You'll always want to make sure your clothes, from top to bottom, make you look and feel your best. Clothing styles change (sometimes rapidly), but there are a few general tips to help you look confident and put-together.

First, you always want to be trendy for your age. Seeing guys, especially older guys, dress from a different decade is absolutely cringe-inducing. If you haven't gone shopping in five years, I promise you that your outfit is not cool anymore.

Second, unless you're gay, be fashionable, but never fashion-forward. In other words, look good in the current styles, but you probably don't want to push it too much in creating new trends.

Third, choose clothes based on your weight and height. Make sure they fit. Avoid clothes that are too baggy or too tight. If you have a big gut, don't wear clothing that accentuates it. Play to your strengths, not your shortcomings.

Finding clothes that fit is harder for short guys and you may have to find a tailor. But, it's worth it. Get your pants hemmed so they don't go down past your shoes. Order smaller sizes online (if needed) if the sizes in the store are too baggy. Have blazers altered so that they don't hang over your hands. Even if you pay a few extra dollars, it's worth it to make your clothes fit properly. You'll look like you care about your appearance and it makes you appear taller.

Fourth, have a formal set of clothes that you can wear occasionally (or regularly). Every guy needs to own a sharp pair of black pants, button down shirt of some type, nice belt, dress shoes, tie (a real one), and blazer. And, they all need to fit. If the occasion arises, you should be able to look professional and dressy. Even if the occasion doesn't arise, find one so you can dress up. Almost every woman I've talked to loves the look of a guy in a suit and tie (and these are women from ages 18-80).

Here are a few other tips for short men:

Avoid pleats. They make you look short and stocky. Always choose straight legged pants.

Avoid horizontal stripes. Only wear vertical ones. Vertical stripes make you look taller; horizontal stripes make you look wider. I think you know which one is best.

Avoid big patterns. If you're going for patterns (like checks, etc.) choose ones that are smaller. Larger ones just draw attention to your small size.

Wear slimming clothes. Looking short and stocky is the last thing you want from a fashion perspective. So, slimming clothing is always preferable (like monochrome color patterns, fewer designs, etc.). Many dress shirts come in different fits. I have found that "slim fit" looks the best on shorter guys because it makes us look taller. If you are not thin enough, then lose weight (see Chapter 15). Pay attention to this type of stuff when choosing clothes.

Your assignment for this chapter is to revamp your wardrobe. If you have the money, hire a fashion consultant and let her help you pick new clothes. A consultant keeps up with the trends and can give you a head start. If you don't have that kind of money, then look at men's magazines and mannequins in the popular stores (and maybe fliers and online catalogs). Then, slowly start to change your wardrobe to reflect the current styles.

The key is to gradually start to make over your appearance. However, you'll have to deal with the hygiene issues immediately. Habits like showering, having clean socks, etc. are basics that everyone should already have mastered. You must start making those a priority starting this second.

Chapter Fourteen

Taking The Elevator

When I was a kid, I watched the movie "Pee-Wee's Big Adventure." No, for those who've missed out on this fine movie, Pee-Wee wasn't a short guy! But, there was a scene where he dances on a bar (no, it's not that type of movie either) after borrowing a guy's shoes. Those shoes must've given Pee Wee six inches! My young mind was shocked that there were heels for men. My dad explained it was a joke because men don't wear heels.

Of course, they don't. At least not heels on the outside.

It wasn't until I was in my thirties that I discovered elevator shoes, or their inserted counterparts, lifts! They can add height up to around four inches! And they're all concealed! What's not to like?! Okay, the exclamation marks are there to show the surprise and excitement that I could add up to four inches to my height! Why…if I added the four inches, I wouldn't just be average! I'd be freaking tall!

Of course, then reality hit me. Yes, I would be four inches taller. But, I was thirty-two years old (at the time). Would anyone really believe I had a four-inch growth spurt at my age? Probably not. Okay, it would at least make me more attractive to women, other men, and potential employers. Of course, once I met them, would I always have to keep my shoes on?

I want to use this chapter to talk about the upsides and pitfalls of using lifts. I'll list a few of each, then tell you what I think is the best solution. So, here goes.

The Upsides

The first upside of using lifts or elevator shoes is obvious: you're taller! I'll bet you never thought that you'd have a growth spurt by paying a few bucks (for lifts) or a little over a hundred (for good elevator shoes). They add instant height, which in our image-obsessed culture is a true upside.

Second, lifts can do amazing things for a guy's confidence. He's more imposing, likely getting more looks from women, and feels secure after years of insecurity. And, that's awesome, especially for short guys who literally might have never even known the joy of being taller than another male human being.

The Downsides

If you're caught up in the euphoria of lifts, then let me burst your bubble a little bit (like when I started asking myself relevant questions). Because, with lifts and elevator shoes, there are definite, very serious, downsides.

The first is this: have you ever tried walking in heels? I think most every guy has, out of curiosity, put on a pair of ladies heels just to give it a go (hopefully in private). Even if you haven't, ask a woman about them. They're hard to walk in, especially ones with the really tall heels.

If you add more than an inch or so, you will essentially be a man wearing high heels. And, they're not added to the foot in a flat way. In order for lifts and elevator shoes to conceal those inches, they literally put them at the heel. Once again, you'll be wearing high heels (just inside). You'll have to learn to walk in them.

Second, ask a woman what high heels do to her legs. Or just look at the research which has shown that heels create a host of problems, ranging from tendonitis, knee degeneration, foot pain, ankle instability, and poor posture. The longer and more consistently a person wears heels, the worse and more varied the side effects become.

Third, if you ever want to get out of your elevator shoes, you're going to look short again. You might not care, but it really will make you look insecure if the situation arises. Don't think the situation won't arise? Think again. There are lots of places where you won't be able to wear lifts, like the beach and the gym. Even wearing shorts is difficult because lifts/elevator shoes require larger shoes and/or boots. And that girl who sees you lose four inches when you step on the elliptical? Yeah, she's going to think that's at the very least a little odd.

Finally, there's always the problem of success. You meet a lovely girl and take her back to your place. You get ready for intimacy. Do you leave your shoes on or lose four inches? Either way you look ridiculous.

So, those are the possible upsides and downsides. While the dream of being tall seems euphoric, the downsides are pretty down. Basically, if you want to wear tall lifts or elevator shoes on a regular basis, you pretty much have to never change shoes, avoid places and activities people enjoy (especially women), and never get intimate without your shoes on.

You might say that lifts are fine for occasional wear, especially when you're out meeting strangers, going to a job interview, etc. This is somewhat true. However, keep in mind your goal for those occasions. For the examples I gave, it's to get a relationship (or even a sexual encounter) or a job. In both cases, you'll be seen one time taller and another time shorter. Does that sort of switch up scream honest or secure? Not really.

Let me add too that lifts represent a double standard. I get it. A woman adds height, it's just dressing up. A man adds it, he's insecure. Once again, it's reality. I don't make the rules, but I'm helping you master them so you can win the game. And, the rules say a man who increases his height in this way is perceived as an insecure loser.

So, you probably think I'm against wearing lifts and/or elevator shoes. I'm actually not. I just think they have to be used carefully and in a certain way.

First of all, I don't recommend adding a lift of more than 1.5 inches. I actually think a half an inch to an inch is about right. That, combined with a shoe with a decent heel, should give you two extra inches or so. That is socially acceptable enough and provides deniability. If someone asks about it, you can just say it's your boots accounting for the height difference. Getting two inches from a normal boot is definitely on the upper end of elevation, but it's plausible. No one is going to believe a normal boot adds four inches.

Second, I'd recommend only wearing them under certain conditions. Job interviews, going to meet women, first dates, networking events, public speaking, etc. come to mind. If you wear them every time you go out or to work every day you're going to start to get the health issues that come from wearing heels.

Practically speaking, you can simply buy one inch inserted lifts and put them in a larger shoe. You can buy shoes that are one size too big if you need to. Buy the lift first, then take it shoe shopping with you. Put it in the shoe, then test it out. Once you buy the shoes, add the lifts, and practice walking. While adding an inch won't affect your walk too much, it's good to get used to them, so your gait is natural.

If you feel that you want to brave the downsides and go taller than an extra inch, more power to you. But, at least you can't say I didn't warn you. My advice, instead of adding fake inches to your height, is to start working on the other tips in this book to increase your value. In the long run, that is going to make you far more successful with women (and in other ways).

This chapter doesn't have an assignment, but, if you decide lifts are for you, at the very least practice walking in them. You don't want to have the extra height advantage, but look like a fool because you can't even walk straight.

CHAPTER FIFTEEN

HEALTH AND PHYSICAL FITNESS

When I was a little kid, I was pretty thin and fit. I was active outdoors and every Sunday after church my friends and I would organize a kickball game in the parking area. However, at the age of eight, something happened. The Nintendo Entertainment System was released and I received one for Christmas. Our Sunday ritual changed from kickball to Super Mario Brothers. Within six months, I was a bona fide fatty.

I hit my (outward) growth spurt at ten. And, since I didn't grow enough upwards, I couldn't compensate for my lack of activity and too many sausage sandwiches. I was a fat preteen and it sucked pretty hard. This was back in the early nineties when most kids were skinny.

My height and weight combined to give me incredibly low self-esteem and, of course, no girlfriends.

Fortunately, I pulled myself together and lost the weight. I did it in eighth grade. It happened because I had become completely sick of being fat and lonely. Much like my journey to popularity and social success, I researched techniques to change my life and correct my shortcomings. In this case, I found out how to eat healthily and workout effectively.

It worked. Although losing weight didn't solve my dating problems long-term, it went a long way towards helping me get the occasional date. And, I felt a ton better about myself.

Now I am very physically fit, skinny, and healthy. All of this is very important to me. And, it should be for every short guy. You don't have to become obsessed about it like I am. But, you do have to care because, remember, as short guys who can't change our heights, we need to do everything else right. One of those things is controlling our weight.

As mentioned previously, having good looks alone won't get you dates. Women prefer a dominant personality to physical traits. So, what role do looks play? First of all, women do appreciate good-looking guys, especially in the initial attraction phases. Few women would be initially attracted to old, ugly rich guys, even though those guys succeed in the end. Still, for the average guy, having the bonus of initial physical attraction with a girl is huge. It sets you apart in the beginning and makes the odds of successfully dating her greater.

Also, physically fit and healthy guys, especially at later ages, are rare, so being fit shows real value the older you get. This is particularly true as society gets fatter and fatter. I guess it's the upside of the obesity epidemic. If you're not just another fat guy, it makes you look that much better by comparison.

Finally, having a good body is a way of feeling better about yourself and gaining confidence. It's much easier to walk into a room with a cocky swagger if you don't have manboobs hanging down to your beer gut.

I'm not going to give a ton of advice on this topic because there are other individuals much more qualified. Also, don't forget to consult with a doctor before starting any diet or exercise plan. You want to make sure that you do them the right and safe way.

<u>Weight Loss</u>

Losing weight is really basic math revolving around calories, specifically calories taken in versus calories burned.

Calories taken in > calories burned = weight gain

Calories taken in < calories burned = weight loss

Calories taken in = calories burned = weight maintenance

So, any diet, no matter what they may tell you, has to account for calories. It's why I also recommend that you count calories in some fashion. There are lots of calorie counting apps and websites. It takes a few minutes each day, but it's well worth it. Studies show that most people dramatically underestimate the calories they consume.

But, all calories aren't created equal. The research seems to show that a diet too high in carbohydrates will lead to the most weight gain. These account for the "empty" calories from foods like potato chips, candy, etc.

Stick to healthy foods like lean meats, fruits, nuts, vegetables and some dairy. Avoid high-sugar foods like candy and pop. In fact, cut out pop altogether. It's just wasted calories. In addition, try to eat a diet high in fiber. Fiber helps keep you regular and makes you feel full. Also, make sure to drink water. It also helps you feel full and it's essential to life.

If you cut your calories and eat healthily, you will lose weight. The average person needs around 2,000 calories a day. So, if you eat close to 2000 calories and do nothing else, you'll likely keep your current weight. If you want to lose weight, then you'll have to cut back on calories (or up your exercise). Don't cut back too much, though, or you'll slow your metabolism (see below).

There is a variable in this discussion called metabolism. This represents your body's processes and how they burn energy (calories). Your metabolism is like the engine of a car. Some cars are gas-guzzlers while others are efficient. You want to be a gas-guzzler. People with higher metabolisms burn more calories per day than those with slower metabolisms. Certain factors (like exercise) can raise metabolism, but a lot of it is genetic. And, it almost always slows with age.

Let me share one final tip related to weight loss. According to The Secrets of Being Happy by Richard Bandler, studies show that vividly recalling a previous meal, by focusing on the way it tasted, smelled, looked, etc., suppresses the appetite. I have found this works too.

Exercise

Another important factor in having a great body is exercise. But, it always must be paired with a healthy diet. Otherwise, you might be in great shape, but you'll have fat covering your amazingly ripped muscles. Here are some exercise tips.

Remember that exercise is simply anything that gets you moving. If it burns calories, it's exercise. A lot of people think in order to exercise they have to buy an Under Armour thermal outfit and start running on the back roads for miles. That's not the case. While running the back roads for miles is great exercise (although who cares about your outfit so long as it works for you), so is walking or even raking leaves.

The first thing you need to do is let go of your stereotypes about exercise, especially if you've hated exercise in the past. Pick an activity that you enjoy and that will get you moving and burning calories.

People often ask me what is the best exercise and I tell them "the one you can stick with." If you hate running, then don't run. If the meatheads at the gym annoy you, then work out at home. Do something that burns calories and keep doing it. It's really that simple.

However, there are a few things that make exercise easier for some people. These might not work for you, but, if you have trouble getting motivated, these tips could help.

The first is to exercise outdoors. For many men and women, this makes physical activity easier or more fun. Personally, I hate running on the treadmill but can easily bust out eight miles in nature. While this is an issue of preference, lots of guys find they enjoy outdoor fitness activities more. Studies also show that while exercise alone can treat mild depression, exercising outside is almost twice as effective as indoor exercise. This is another reason to burn calories outside (see lifeinyouryears.net/blog/2009/06/30/some-thoughts-on-exercise-and-mood).

Second, find a sport to play. Fitness doesn't have to be elliptical machines and weight-lifting. Any sport can get you in amazing shape, especially if you enjoy it. Hours can fly by and in some cases you might not even know it. Find a basketball league, play some pick-up football, get out on the tennis courts, etc. If you like a sport, then play it.

Third, listen to music. Studies have shown that music helps people exercise longer. If you are doing an activity that isn't the most exciting, adding some music to the mix should help you last longer and make your exercise more intense.

Finally, exercise with someone else. Working out with a partner serves a couple purposes. Number one, it helps because it keeps you distracted. Talking to a buddy or just having someone there keeps your mind off the fact that you're exercising. Second, a friend can be a good motivator. David and I like to run together because we push each other to work harder. In the same vein, some guys find the social atmosphere of a gym helps them accomplish more.

Motivation

Whatever exercise or dieting plan you pick, it's vital that you stick with it. You'll ultimately have to change long-term habits if you want to keep your new body very long. Anyone can lose a few pounds or work out for a couple of weeks. But, you'll have to form long-term habits if you really want your new self to become an integral part of your life.

I've been eating right and exercising for nearly fifteen years. It hasn't always been the easiest, but I manage to stay motivated through it all. I keep my plan because I value the way I look when I'm thin. I don't keep fat pictures or my old pants around (although I do have a mental image of my fat college body).

I typically motivate myself by asking a variation of a single question: would I rather do "x" or be thin? For example, if I'm tempted to eat a giant piece of cake, I'll ask myself, "Would I rather have this cake or be thin?" or "Would I rather sit on my butt watching TV or be thin?" I know how much I love being thin. It always wins out.

Of course, it's good to splurge on food occasionally (life's too short) and your body needs days off. But, whenever I feel I'm making an excuse, I ask myself that simple question. I always value having a good body over eating junk or skipping a workout. I'm proud of what I do and will continue to do it. It's a big motivating factor for me.

Your assignment is to take your body's measurements. Buy a measuring tape and measure your neck, chest, arms, waist, hips, and legs. Also, weigh yourself. Now, you are going to start a diet and exercise plan. If you already have one and are fit, then don't worry about changing it. If you don't, then it's time to start.

Find a website or app where you can track your calories. Cut back on junk food and keep your calories at a level where you will start to lose some weight. Find activities that you will enjoy. Play a sport, go to the gym, run around your neighborhood, etc. And, actually do it! Unless something (like a condition) prevents you, you should ideally work out four to five days a week. Keep track of your activities as well.

Remember to talk to a doctor before doing any of this. You might find it beneficial to consult with a weight loss and/or fitness professional as well. A nutritionist can help you lose weight and a personal trainer can assist you with exercise techniques and motivation.

Every two weeks weigh in and measure yourself. You might want to take "before" photos too. Hopefully, if you create and stick with a plan, you'll see the numbers on the scale fall and the inches decrease.

Remember, however, that muscle weighs more than fat. So, what you see on the tape measure is much more important than the scale, especially if you are doing weight lifting or other resistance type exercises.

Hopefully you will see your physical appearance improve. It's not the only factor, but it will go a long way in boosting your self-esteem and increasing your initial attraction with women.

Chapter Sixteen

Low-Value Stuff

I follow a guy on social media who seems like a good guy, but it's obvious that he's pretty much dateless. It's easy to see why when you look at his Facebook posts. He's always sharing his love for girly movies (and other things) and he talks a lot about his toy collection. There's nothing wrong with collecting toys as an adult, but always mentioning it online doesn't exactly scream high-value to women (who want to date a man). Oh, and before you ask, he is tall, proving that even tall men can lose at the dating game.

Since I've gone through some high-value traits and accomplishments, I want you to be aware of the opposite: low-value traits and activities that can make you lose points when trying to win over women.

Keep in mind that opinions differ. So, one girl's "low-value" may be acceptable to another girl. But, in general, women think and act in similar ways. So, yes, you can probably find a girl on Tumblr who likes a certain trait or fetish (like a toy-collecting man). But, it doesn't prove much of anything. If you want dates, you'll have to go with the odds. And, in general, what I discuss below is considered low-value across the board.

First, I want to talk about the lowest of low-value behavior, which is being creepy. If you do creepy things, then hang it up. Being creepy is a total deal-breaker with all but the weirdest women. Creepy behavior makes women feel uncomfortable and even afraid. They feel this visceral fear as an evolutionary response to a perceived threat to their safety. If they're afraid of you, you're not getting any action, I promise you.

I've included more about creepiness in the next chapter. So, I'm not going to discuss it much here. But, be aware that if you're creepy, you'll come across as the ultimate low-value guy, and be dateless because of it.

Okay, let's assume you're not creepy. What other ways can you come across as low-value? Here are a few of the major ones.

Being Perceived As Girly

Remember, most women want a powerful, masculine provider and protector. They don't want a guy who acts just like them (in other words, girly). They will hang around with girly guys, but they usually like them only as friends.

Lots of guys fall for the myth that acting like girls is a ticket to get "in their pants." So, a guy will profess his love for "Twilight" or pretend to be super sensitive. After all that work being girly, he then wonders why he gets friend-zoned. It's because women are friends with other girls. They don't date them. They date men, usually masculine ones.

So, don't be perceived as having girly interests. Seek out masculine activities like sports, shooting, etc. Don't be afraid to express those interests. If she tells you about a great chick flick, it's okay to say you're not interested in seeing it or even discussing it with her. She'll likely think you're more attractive for doing it!

If you have girly interests or like feminine things, then branch out from those. Ditch the collection of miniature figurines (or at least don't talk about them so much) and take an interest in the NFL instead. Quit talking so much about your love of "Twilight" and instead read up on Earnest Hemingway. You get the point. Think being manlier isn't "you?" Well, I've got bad news: "you" will likely be single.

Putting Women On A Pedestal

This is also a huge mistake guys make. They put women on a pedestal and treat them like princesses or even goddesses. And, this is before they even get the first date! These guys buy girls drinks, pay for expensive meals, and go out of their way to compliment them, even before they know any attraction exists. Yet, inevitably these women date jerks instead! Oh, the horror and the pain of being a nice guy!

The reasons these nice guys lose out to assholes is because putting women on a pedestal doesn't make you look masculine. It makes you look subservient, not like a strong provider and protector.

And, as much as women will enjoy the attention, and gladly take your free stuff, they won't have sex with you, date you, or be your boyfriend. They'll save that for the guy who is masculine. See…now it makes sense why all that money you spent on those girls didn't make them more attracted to you!

It's cool to be nice to a girl and even be generous. However, before you are sure she is attracted to you, we advise you be generous at the levels you would with your guy-friends. Would you buy your guy-friend a coffee or a small meal? Yes. Would you buy him a meal at a five-star restaurant followed by a dozen roses? I'd hope not!

If you're already dating the girl and getting what you want from her, then by all means, buy her dinner and take good care of her. But, don't think that wining and dining a girl who's not attracted to you is going to get you action. If a horribly ugly girl bought you a gift, would you date her? Probably not. It's the same way with women. You can't bribe them into being attracted to you.

Kissing Up

This is related to putting women on a pedestal, except this is specifically about guys who are super agreeable with women. They think they have to always affirm women and agree with their opinions or else women will lose romantic interest in them.

In reality, the opposite is true. Women like strong and confident guys, remember? You can show your strength and confidence by being yourself and standing up for your beliefs. Don't be an off-putting jerk or challenge her like you would some guy on an Internet forum discussion. But, you should calmly and humorously assert your beliefs if the chance arises. Or calmly and humorously disagree. In fact, when I meet a new girl, I try to disagree with her at least once, even if it's as simple as saying, "That's not really my cup of tea."

Look at most couples you know, do they agree on absolutely everything? Of course not! Don't think you have to kiss up and agree all the time. If you do agree, then by all means express it. But, if you don't agree, express it too.

I know many guys who, in hopes of getting a date, have listened to a girl's every problem, affirming every bad relationship choice she has made, only to be passed over in favor of the very guys she was complaining about! Agreeing all the time is never a good idea.

And, as I mentioned in a previous chapter, never apologize unless you did something wrong. For example, if a girl isn't paying attention and bumps into you, don't say, "I'm sorry." You didn't do anything to merit that. Instead say something funny and confident like, "That was a nice block; you could play fullback for the Patriots!"

Neediness

I once watched a grown man break down into tears and beg a girl to date him in public. It was at a coffee shop and she had just told him that she didn't want to see him anymore. After his emotional outburst, he stormed out angry. I talked to the young woman and asked her how long they had been dating. She said, "A week!"

I laughed and asked, "Too needy?"

She laughed. "Waaaaay too needy"

Does needing a girlfriend for fulfillment sound like the trait of a confident and powerful provider? Absolutely not. While it's normal and acceptable to rely on others and enjoy their emotional company, that's much different from needing another human being to be complete.

A man should be independent enough to function and remain confident without a woman on his side. That kind of aloof attitude is actually what attracts a woman. If she is the one providing and protecting a needy man, the roles are reversed. She's not wired to desire this type of relationship, and I guarantee she will eventually get rid of you or cheat with more confident guys.

So, if you absolutely need a woman or get needy when you date one, you're going to be single more often than not. Re-read the chapter on detachment for tips to stop needing women so much (see Chapter 9). Find hobbies and accomplishments and raise your self-esteem without a woman.

Being Whiny or Angry

Back in college, David was having a particularly bad night out. This was before we transformed our lives and he was frustrated about his lack of success with women. We were out trying to have a good time, but all David did was whine and complain.

He was angry and I can't blame him. He acted out of frustration and we all feel frustrated at times. However, do you think that David's whiny, angry attitude was going to win him any dates that night? Nope! He got into a negative feedback loop of anger and whining and no woman wanted anything to do with him. He went home that night more single than when he left!

As short men, we have a lot to be angry about. And, a lot to complain about. But, guess what it will accomplish? Absolutely nothing. Actually, take that back. It will just make you more unattractive. So, when you're out, at work, etc., don't whine and complain. It makes you look insecure and unattractive.

This also includes those of you who are more activistic. Even if you want to save the whales or end something outrageous, focus on the inspiring aspects of what you're doing to make positive change rather than cultivating outrage. It may seem useful to always complain about the negatives. And, there are many negatives in the world. But, after a while that negativity wears thin on all but the most committed ideologues.

Focus on the positives in your life and talk about those in your social environments. It has a couple benefits. First, it makes you look high-value because you're focusing on what you do well. Second, it helps others know more about you (self-promotion). That's always a good thing.

Self Loathing

I recently talked to a few short guys, just to get the sense of what should be in this book (outside of my own experience as a short man). As they opened up about their situations, I discovered something interesting. Nearly all of them hated their height. A couple even admitted that they hated themselves because they were short.

This is called self-loathing and it typically occurs when a person hates himself because of some trait, usually one that he can't change. There are self-loathing Jews, blacks, short men, women, etc. Hating yourself is the most low-value trait of all for a man. There's no way a man who hates his core being can ever project anything but shame, low-value, and bitterness to everyone else.

Short guys have often come to hate their height because it has caused them so many issues over the years. Bullying, being picked last at sports, getting no attention from women, etc., can lead to resentment, especially if the frustration continues for a long time. It's natural to resent a trait (height) that leads to that.

But, if you loathe yourself, you'll just come across as perpetually angry, bitter, and lacking in confidence. And, this is not going to win affection from anyone, male or female. A person like this may luck into a date, but isn't going to stay in a relationship very long.

Women may give you attention if you come across this way. But I promise you, it will just result from the pity they feel for you. You may get a few texts that start with "aww…" but they will date your more confident buddies.

If you are self-loathing because of your height, you'll have to get over it. It's easier said than done, I know. The first step is to at least see your height as neutral. I don't love the fact that I'm short. However, I don't hate it either. To me, my height just "is," like the width of my nose or structure of my hands. You'll need to get to that point in your life too.

One way to get rid of a self-loathing attitude is to find and create high-value accomplishments. Create a reason to love yourself! It helps you realize that things you hate about yourself (like height) aren't as important as your awesome accomplishments. But, you have to earn some of these accomplishments and share them with the world.

This list is not exhaustive, so don't think you've gotten off easy if the previous examples don't apply to you. But, this should at least help you avoid low-value behavior that will hinder you from getting dates and staying in relationships. Of course, you'll actually have to make the changes, which brings us to your assignment.

I'd like you to list some of your low-value feelings and behaviors. Use the examples from this chapter as a guide. A good way to identify these behaviors is to ask yourself, "If someone else acted this way, would I perceive him as low value?"

Then, list some action steps to stop doing the behaviors. Here's a hint: most of the solutions relate to getting real accomplishments and raising your self-esteem.

Chapter Seventeen

Don't Be Creepy

A guy I grew up with once bragged on his Facebook page how he bullied a guy into committing suicide. The guy who killed himself had just done a pretty bad thing. But, publicly admitting that he drove another human being to suicide was pretty creepy. Then again, this dude has a long history of creepiness, which started with borderline stalking girls in elementary school.

Being creepy means you create a feeling of uneasiness in others. It isn't just what you say that can be creepy. Your looks, mannerisms, body language, dress, gestures, etc. can also make other people feel ill-at-ease. Creepiness is sometimes in the eye of the beholder. However, in general, creepiness, for the vast majority of people, is a lot like how

Supreme Court Justice Potter Stewart defined pornography: you know it when you see it.

Being creepy sends out a bad vibe. It says you are weird, have low-value, and even worse, that you may be dangerous. As mentioned previously, you may have everything going for you, but being creepy will invalidate all your other advantages. Picking up on creepy behavior is likely an evolutionarily developed trait. Our subconscious minds pick up that the creepy person is different and possibly dangerous. And, it tells the brain to be extra cautious.

This is why women often don't even know why they find a guy creepy. They just know he creeps them out for some reason. Likely, they are picking up something subtle in the way he acts that is alerting the older parts of their brains that something isn't quite right.

If you think you may be creepy, don't get the notion that you can master every technique in this book and still get a date. Someone who is creepy, but gains confidence, just becomes even creepier, like a creep on steroids.

A lady I know has a friend who is filthy rich and handsome, yet he's always single. He cries when he's drunk at parties because he feels guilty about having sex with call-girls. In other words, he may be rich, but no female in her right mind wants to be around him (unless he pays them). You might master everything in this book, but if you act in a socially unacceptable way, even occasionally, you'll still likely be single. So, keep your weird hobbies to yourself.

If anything in this chapter sounds like you, or if you've been called creepy before, keep reading. It is absolutely essential that you lose the creepy vibe immediately. Since you may have been creepy your entire life, being non-creepy could require work, but like every other problem you face in this book, it's not impossible to change your behavior.

The first step is to be self-aware. You must be able to understand your thoughts, actions, and how your thoughts influence your actions. You need to be aware how your body language and words come across to other people.

Second, get some feedback from friends and acquaintances and act on the feedback. Go out with some guys that you know are not creepy, and have them take a look at how you interact with people. If they see anything creepy, have them tell you. Some creepy behavior may be accidental, like an off-hand comment or gesture, but other things you do and say might be regular creepy occurrences, and it is important that you know it. You can also model these non-creepy friends. Watch their limits especially.

The difference between charming and creepy hinges usually on what is "not said." This is because while everyone has occasional abnormal thoughts and impulses, creepy people typically share those publicly and even act on them. You must learn to develop a filter.

Keep in mind a few topics that typically make most people uncomfortable: death, rape, violence, sexual aggression, fetishes, etc. If it's rated NC-17 or you have to be eighteen to learn more about it on the internet, it's best to avoid it in conversation, especially when dealing with total strangers. Even with friends, you probably don't want to bring up your deviancy. Better still, stop being so creepily deviant!

Finally, change creepy behavior. If you're going to succeed you'll have to learn to self-censor and get rid of those old patterns. This will come over time, by taking control of your thoughts and constantly modeling other people for appropriateness. If you can't shake the creepy mentality, you'll possess a bunch of positive traits, but one seemingly small hindrance will invalidate them all. Your brain can be re-wired and you'll have to get those non-creepy neurons firing.

If you fail the creepy test, your homework is to write out an action plan to stop being creepy based on my tips in this chapter. If you aren't creepy, then give yourself a hand. The world has one less oddball to deal with!

Chapter Eighteen

What About Napoleon?

One time in junior high, I was getting a little bossy with my classmates during discussion about a group project. Okay…I was a lot bossy. After a few days of my dictatorial style, one of the other guys looked at me and said, "My dad told me to tell you to cool it, Napoleon." I had no clue what he was talking about, but went home and researched Napoleon.

It was only after reading the entry on Napoleon that I discovered the source of his father's comment: the Napoleon complex. This is an alleged sense of inferiority that short guys feel due to their lack of height. That inferiority complex causes them to be dictatorial and bossy, allegedly to compensate for their lack of verticality.

Let's get a couple of things straight. Yes, Napoleon was short. But, he was of an average height for his day. So, he likely wasn't compensating for any physical shortcoming. Which brings us to the second point: maybe he was just a power hungry dick. That's what it's called when a person is of an average or taller height. This is a low-value trait that deserves its own chapter. This is a book for short guys after all.

I think there are short men who get Napoleon complexes. Hell, I probably did have one in seventh grade because I'm sure the power went to my head. I certainly didn't have any power on the sports field or at parties. Perhaps you aren't even in a position of power. Still, you should be putting yourself in leadership positions. And, even if you are a good, fair, compelling leader, it's only a matter of time before someone pulls out the Napoleon card.

As a short guy who finds success, you're going to be judged more harshly. You'll also likely be subject to a lot more scrutiny. This is for a couple of reasons. The main one is that whiny, petty people often look for a reason to bring down others, especially successful people. It could be height or anything else they can find. Also, if you become more of a leader and take more risks, then you're likely going to piss people off. And, when you do, they'll grasp at anything. So, you'll be Napoleon.

You'll have to make sure to keep your cool and not let the criticism bother you. Hey, when you were nobody, it didn't matter. If you're truly improving your life, you'll have to do what the best of the best always do: ignore the criticism and let it roll off you. Definitely don't turn into a micromanaging dictator. It will hinder your success with men and women. Plus, we successful short guys don't need any blowhards out there perpetuating stereotypes.

Another point worth mentioning is that fear of being labeled insecure should never influence your decisions, whether in dating or otherwise. You should always do what you think is right and high-value. It's like in the previous paragraph. You don't want to act like a dictator because that's wrong and low-value.

If you fear being labeled insecure, then guess what that says about you? Yep, it tells everyone you're insecure. You'll start hedging your positions and wimping out. Even if your decision or action ends up being wrong, if it seems like the right thing to do after deliberation, just do it and own it. Anything done confidently enough can appear to be the truth anyway.

If someone accuses you of acting like Napoleon, keep a couple of things in mind. First, if they throw out the reference, you're not likely not dealing with an idiot. That's a good thing. Second, you'll need to have a witty comeback. I like to take the conversation away from height. I say something like, "Yeah, we do share a lot in common. Like him, I'm a powerful guy who gets all the ladies I want. But, I haven't conquered most of Europe...yet."

You don't really have an assignment for this chapter, except to be aware of the Napoleon complex label and to expect it to be thrown out at times. This is especially true once you start changing for the better and taking positions of leadership.

I was probably right to be called out for being such a jerk in junior high. Of course, it's not like I needed anything to add to my height related insecurity. It's too bad I didn't have a book like this to steer me in the right direction. After all, Napoleon did get a lot of action from women. But, he also got exiled (and maybe syphilis). Still, I'm sure it was a small price to pay for conquering all of Europe.

Chapter Nineteen

Self-Promotion

I was raised to be very humble. And, that's not necessarily a bad thing in a world filled with annoying "attention whores." But, combined with a period of low self-esteem due to my height and weight, I became very reluctant to be proud of and excited about my value and accomplishments. But, it's hard to get others excited and thinking about my high-value when I'm not willing to project it.

Many short guys have fallen into the same trap. They have become so used to being beaten down and passive, that they don't know how to promote themselves or share how great they are. If this is you, then you'll absolutely need to read this chapter. You can become incredibly high-value using the previously mentioned tips (or by avoiding the pitfalls of the last few chapters), but you also have to share that value with the world.

First, don't presume that others know how great you are. Lots of passive guys assume that their talents and valuable traits will be manifestly obvious to others. From my personal experience, in most cases, people won't know your value unless you share it. I worked at a private school and was very good at my job. But, I never bragged or shared my accomplishments. When I was let go after a few years, I think it was in part because I just passively let others define me.

You may think people are aware of the details of your life, but the truth is that they probably aren't. Your boss is likely too busy with life, or too busy worrying about his own accomplishments, to notice the great things you are doing.

Second, you'll have to be more extroverted. If you feel the time is right to talk about yourself, you'll have to develop the ability to do it. This goes for business and dating. So, if a girl mentions she loves guys who play guitar, it's time to brag about your mad guitar skills.

Third, you'll have to take a more philanthropic approach to what you do. If you have high-value traits, then people really will want to get to know you and appreciate those traits. Let's look at a great singer. There are many people who would probably love to hear him sing. By singing in public and sharing his abilities, he's meeting people's needs. If you are valuable and you refuse to promote that value, then you are cheating people out of great experiences!

Take this view when you're out on dates. You are a high-value guy (or are becoming one). You need to project this reality to women and let them know it. They want to date a high-value guy, so you are giving them exactly what they want. And, you obviously get something in return too! This insight came from Elizabeth Cobey-Piper at Affinity Matchmaking/Dating Directions. I want to publicly thank her for this!

You'll want to talk about yourself and your accomplishments in a natural way. Breaking out a list of your awesomeness to read on a date will only make you look like a tool. The best thing you can do is to throw out your value in subtle ways in the normal conversation, after you have built genuine rapport, so it doesn't look like you're bragging. But, if there is an opening and it's contextual, be sure to talk about yourself. You'll always want to follow-up, however, with conversation topics that get the girl talking about herself too.

Let's look at an example. The conversation moves towards how she went to the gym in the morning before your date. You can ask her what workouts she did. Then, when she explains her routines, you can throw in your fitness accomplishments, like maybe how you run several miles a day or how you've completed several mud races.

Another tip is to always center the conversation on how your accomplishments make you feel. First, women love that kind of emotionally relevant language. Second, it sounds less like bragging and more like sharing your thoughts. For example, you could say, "I run several miles every morning. I just love the way the fresh air feels. It really starts my day right."

Notice how that statement really is bragging, but the last two sentences soften the bragging. The girl won't think you're a blowhard, but the accomplishment is still noted in her subconscious brain and makes you look attractive. This is bragging without her even thinking you're bragging!

So, make sure that you have value and promote it to others. Straddle the fine line between not discussing your accomplishments and bragging and you'll successfully communicate how great you are to women. This can even work in business and other settings, as well.

You've already listed your accomplishments (Chapter 7). You should be creating new ones too, as you reach your goals. Now, pick a couple and go out and brag about them to someone, preferably someone you're attracted to it. Do it using the tips listed above.

I'd also like you to resolve to talk more about yourself and your accomplishments, with everyone, not just women. It will let others know how awesome you are and start getting you a reputation for being a talented and accomplished person. Don't let yourself go unnoticed. Like many short guys, you've probably been doing that your whole life. What good has it done?

Chapter Twenty

Learn A New Language

In lower primates, the alpha male, who pretty much gets all the females, is often the largest primate in the colony. The same is true of humans. CEOs are much taller on average than the typical American man. According to the National Geographic Channel series "Going Ape," over seventy percent of CEOs are over six feet tall, a number far higher than that of the general male population.

That seems like bad news for short guys, and at first glance, it is. But among apes and other primates, a smaller primate can be the alpha male if he modifies his body language. Yes, alpha male primates "strut their stuff" and have a unique walk that beta primates lack. But, a smaller primate can change his body language and become the boss.

The most successful short guys I have known at dating have had pristine body language. With every ounce of their being, from the eyes down to the feet, they telegraph confidence. Suddenly, their height doesn't matter anymore. I include myself and my brother in this category.

From our understanding of lower animals, this makes perfect sense. David came up with a radical hypothesis a while ago. He argues that women aren't really after tall guys per se. What women seek, like their female primate cousins, is testosterone, or more accurately, guys with it. The scientific evidence suggests this as well.

The reason tall guys are initially more attractive to women is that height and muscle size in men are signs of having testosterone. Thus, women's brains evolved to see height as a kind of "shortcut" indicator that a guy is manly, and thus a provider and protector. So, a short guy standing next to a tall guy will always be at an *initial* disadvantage. However, this is where body language comes in.

Like the smaller, but more dominant, lower primate who ends up outgunning the bigger guy, changing your body language not only telegraphs confidence, but can even boost testosterone levels. I am not going to go into complete body language modulation here. That could be an entire book.

I do want to go over some basics so you can telegraph you are the boss and possess what is attractive to both men and women. I have included some photos at the end that should help.

First, own your space. This means being relaxed, comfortable, and even physically spread out. So if you're sitting at your desk, don't hunch up all tight. Open up. Spread your things out. When sitting at a table in public, take up a little more space than usual. Also, be as relaxed as possible. I guarantee you are relaxed at home (because you own it). Act just as relaxed anywhere you go.

Second, take your time. There is a reason uptight guys are usually portrayed as moving quickly, because rapidly shuffling is a nervous trait. If you own a space, you spend more time in it, which means you move slowly. Think of what it means to have "swagger"; part of it is walking more slowly. A confident guy isn't in a hurry to get anywhere.

Third, make (and keep) eye contact. In the animal kingdom, breaking eye contact shows submission. Dominant males naturally make more eye contact. Always make eye contact with everyone you meet.

We suggest making eye contact with a woman and holding it until she breaks it. Women are much better at making eye contact than men. This is a sex difference that is seen even among infants. Women expect a guy to hold eye contact. Even if it is awkward, make her break it first.

Fourth, make yourself look bigger. Stick your chest out a little. Stand up straighter. When you walk, strut a little. Size does matter in physical domination, and enlarging yourself works to telegraph how confident you are, especially if you're shorter.

Fifth, avoid body blocking. Body blocking is placing something between you and the person you are interacting with. It could be crossed arms, a bottle of beer, or a table. Visit a club some time and watch how many guys have a beer glued to their chest. That is body blocking, and it is your subconscious mind putting a barrier between you and what makes you nervous.

People do it in front of crowds a lot, by standing with their arms folded across their lower abdominal area. Rarely do people stand like this when they are at home. This is called "crotch blocking" and is our brain's attempt at protecting our vital reproductive organs.

You can counter this tendency by always holding drinks at your side, and making sure your chest is exposed. Notice that military and police officers almost always stand with their chests unguarded, and their hands behind their back. When you stand in this position, you are subconsciously telling people, "Hey, look at me, I am so confident I can leave my vital organs wide open." You may laugh, but it's true!

Sixth, avoid submissive gestures. A major one is exposing your palms, often combined with a shrug of the shoulders. If a woman calls you out on something ridiculous, and you do that, you are telling her how weak you are.

There might be a time for these gestures (in times when you genuinely want to be submissive, like if a boss is ripping you), but if you use them a lot, you are constantly telegraphing submission.

Finally, you need to use your body language to increase your testosterone. My guess is that all of what I have mentioned above boosts your testosterone. However, studies have shown that certain poses definitely raise it. I am going to explain those below. However, first I want to remind you of an important related concept called "fake it 'til you make it," which I have already mentioned.

At first, these poses may seem awkward, and not "you." Physiologically speaking (i.e. your testosterone levels) you probably aren't confident. However, like I just said, changing your body language actually increases testosterone.

Thus, "faking" confident body language eventually convinces your body that you are confident. After doing this for a while, these moves will come naturally to you, because your testosterone levels will be elevated.

This creates a cool feedback loop where confident body language leads to more confidence which leads to more confident body language, and so forth. So, the lesson is do the poses, even if they don't feel natural at first.

Let me get back to the poses. These poses were used in a study by Carney, Cuddy, and Yap of Harvard University to boost testosterone levels. Sit in a chair in front of a table or desk. Lean back and prop your feet up on the table. Place your hands behind your head so your elbows stick out to the sides of your head.

The other pose studied is to simply stand over a table or desk and place your hands on the desk, spreading your arms out as wide as possible (i.e. taking up space…that should sound familiar).

According to the study, holding these poses for a few minutes a day was all that was needed to boost testosterone. I suggest holding each for a few minutes a day in private, or using them before big events or going out to meet women.

Your assignment is to give your body language an overhaul. Gradually fix it based on the lessons in this chapter. Introduce some of the tips into your life over the next few weeks. Try to learn and practice a new one each day if you can. This gradual process will make the change more comfortable for you and less "obvious" to those around you.

Eventually, you will notice that women just look at you more. Since women love guys with higher testosterone, there is probably something subconscious going on. They may not even know they are staring. Either way, start changing your body language today!

What follows are some photos illustrating some of the various tips I provide. Consult them if you are having trouble visualizing some of the poses.

Here is an example of body blocking with a drink. This shows insecurity. Hold the drink by your side instead.

This is pleading and shows submission. Guys that sport this look are saying, "You win!"

This is a pose similar to that used in the testosterone boosting study. Hold poses like this to increase your confidence.

This is the second pose studied that boosts testosterone. Notice the arms are spread out very wide, taking up space.

Chapter Twenty-One

Read Her Body Language To Read Her Mind

After one of our speaking events, David and I went out for some wings. We did one of our typical routines on the waitress, joking that we were mystery shoppers. We were having a really good evening and were super-confident.

Of course, we always are checking to see if our methods are effective (we view our routines scientifically; if they don't work, we revise them or get rid of them). After she left our table she did a little dance, with a spring in her step. She was smiling and laughing the rest of the night, and kept stopping by our table without any good reason.

We never have to ask a girl if we are "wowing" her. She tells us, not with words, but with body language. Skipping? Smiling? Coming back around? Yeah, she was enjoying the interaction.

Some of our clients have trouble determining if their interactions with women are having a positive or negative impact. Fortunately, a woman's body language is a great indicator of what she is thinking and feeling. You probably always wanted the ability to read a woman's mind. Now you can!

In this chapter I want to give you some basic body language cues women send out. This will give you more insight into what women think about you, and provide great feedback about whether a particular line, personal change, etc., is having a positive or negative effect on them. It is also a great way to know if they are attracted to you or not.

Most body language is sent out subconsciously. People may not even know they are doing it. Just as in the last chapter I pointed out that you may have been telling the world that you were insecure for years without even realizing it, unless people read a book like this, they are probably just as unaware of their body language. This is good for you. It means that they are probably revealing a lot about themselves and don't even know it.

This chapter is not an all-out lesson on reading female body language. However, it will give you enough basics to get by, and allow you to have a good base for learning more.

Women give out what we call "Signs of Attraction" ("SOAs" from here on out). Humans are animals, right? We send out signs of sexual interest just like birds, ferrets, and insects. You know all those insect sounds you hear on a summer night? That is them sending out sounds that tell other insects they are ready for sex. Even with our advanced brains, we still send out similar signals.

Women may send out signals of interest and not even know they are doing it. Their true feelings of attraction, expressed via body language, may even contradict what they are thinking in the more advanced parts of their brains. So, keep in mind just because the older parts of her brain are telling her you're hot doesn't mean her frontal lobe isn't thinking, "I don't have time for a guy." So, an SOA isn't necessarily a guarantee of a date, sex, or anything else.

Also, you must know that sometimes women do these things out of habit, or for other reasons. They could even have another guy in mind instead you. One SOA isn't a guarantee of anything. We tell our clients to look for an overall pattern.

First, a general rule to remember is that people point to what they like, and away from what they don't. I can tell I have a woman's attention when her naval and feet are pointed toward me. These are the best indications of interest. If you are talking to a woman, and one or more of her feet are pointed away, that indicates she wants to get away. If you have been making eye contact with a girl, and her naval is toward you, that is a good sign she is thinking about you.

Second, another general rule is that people close themselves off to things they don't like, and open themselves up to what they like. If you are talking to her and she crosses her arms and stops smiling (closing the mouth), you have probably blown it. If she opens up, then you are doing well.

Third, the farther away from the head, the more "honest" the body part will be. It is easy to lie to people with your face, but harder with your feet. Feet are a great indicator of honesty. When I was running at my local YMCA, the track was set up so the swimming pools were visible below. One day I saw a female lifeguard sitting high up on her chair, interacting with a male lifeguard below her. Her legs were dangling. They were swinging wildly with excitement. She may have been playing it cool with her words and facial expressions, but her legs gave away her attraction to that guy. By the way, the legs moving like that are a sign of happiness and/or attraction.

Fourth, if a woman exposes certain areas of her body to you, it shows possible attraction. Of course, if she shows you her boobs then, yeah, that's obvious! That's not what I'm referring to. If your dog or cat trusts you, what does he do? He shows you his stomach. A woman isn't likely to roll around on the ground and show you her stomach (but if she does, she definitely likes you!). However, she will often expose her neck and wrist to you. These are locations of major arteries, and exposing them is saying, "I trust you."

Have you ever walked behind a woman and she flipped up her hair and revealed her neck? That is an SOA, because she is saying, "I'm vulnerable and open to interaction with you."

Fifth, women will often "check you out." Like a guy, they will do a quick "up and down" with their eyes. If they like you, they will make sure you see them doing it.

Sixth, they will flip their hair. There are a few reasons they do this. One reason is that guys have evolved to notice things in motion more so than stationary things. In the jungle, men were the tribe's hunters. We needed to notice moving things to survive. When women flip their hair for you, they are getting your attention in the main way we notice things. Also, thick and long hair is a sign of health and fertility in a woman, which is why men are attracted to women with long hair. By flipping it, she is making it look even more thick and flowing.

Seventh, women will touch you if they like you. They will gently touch your arm, face, leg, or chest. Sometimes, if you are flirting, she will make the contact harder, usually under the guise of faux-outrage.

Eighth, a woman will give you a genuine and full smile if she likes you. Women smile more than men, and don't always mean something sexual by it, but nonetheless, if a woman smiles around you a lot, she probably feels something romantic for you. If she scowls a lot, then chances are she is either generally mean or doesn't like you very much.

Finally, let me spend some time talking about the eyes. A great indicator of attraction, which cannot be consciously controlled to any real extent, is dilated (open) pupils. If a woman's pupils are dilated when talking to you, it is a good SOA. Also, women love eye contact. If they are interested, they will make sustained eye contact. Often they will tilt their head slightly and give you a deep gaze.

I am going to throw in one more point that relates to body language, and it is what we call an "SOA Mandate." Approaching women can be challenging. Knowing what you know about body language, we believe that any time you get a solid SOA, you should say something to that girl. Even if her conscious mind isn't sure, you have a good idea some part of her likes you. This is a good way to gain confidence in approaching women, because you are reading the signs before approaching, giving you an edge from a "cold" approach.

Your assignment is to go out to a busy environment and watch women. Examine their interactions with guys. Observe their behavior when they like a guy and when they don't. Look at some of the points in this chapter and observe them in action. Also, in your interactions with everyone, consciously pay attention to body language. The more you pay attention, the more you will become an expert. Eventually you will be able to know what women are thinking before they even say a word.

The next few pages contain some images of how women show attraction. Study these photos.

She is smiling and exposing the wrist. This is a good sign that she may be attracted to you.

This is a hair flip and neck exposure combination. The flip gets your attention, and exposing the neck shows that she feels safe and secure around you.

This girl is bored and thus closed to interaction. If you are talking to her and you observe this body language, you aren't exactly "wowing" her.

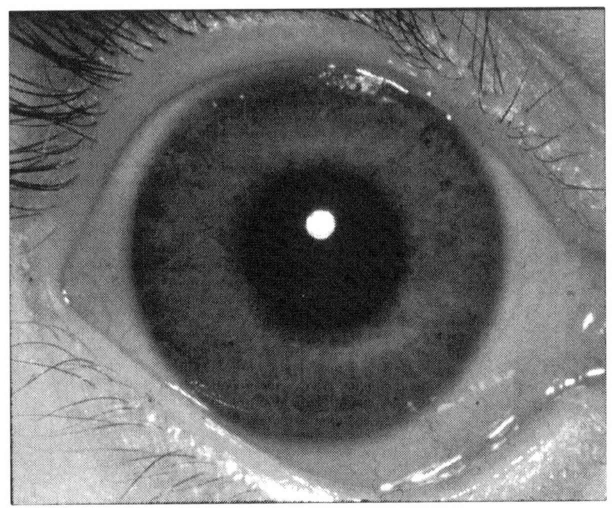

This pupil is fairly dilated (i.e. expanded). I have seen eyes even more dilated than this when someone has been attracted to me.

Chapter Twenty-Two

Don't Believe Her...Observe Her

I had a friend who kept a list with all of the traits of her "perfect guy." When asked about it, she would gladly rattle off every characteristic her prince charming absolutely had to have. He "had" to be tall, sweet, have a good job, and earn a college degree, among other things. When she started to become close to different guys, she would mention the list, and most guys knew they couldn't meet all of these standards, and gave up.

So did my friend end up marrying her prince charming? I have no idea. What I do know is that through her college years at least, when I knew her, she dated jerk after jerk and loser after loser. Almost every guy she dated had nearly *zero* of the traits on her list. That's right: zero!

So, why am I mentioning this story in a book about short guys getting a date? The reason is that when women write down what they want in a guy, guess what is almost always included in the list? Yep, a guy who is tall.

To a shorter man, this is depressing to hear. You think a woman is interested, or that you are getting along well, and suddenly you hear her tell her friends (or you directly) of her height standards. Since many shorter guys are already insecure, this revelation can lead to anger, bitterness, and even preemptively cutting off the relationship.

After years of observing the behavior of both men and women, and studying the science behind attraction, I can safely say that regarding relationship preferences, I rarely believe what a woman (or man) says. Let me explain why.

As I mention frequently on our website, attraction is *not* an intellectual choice. Attraction "happens" in the older parts of our brains, namely in the parts classified (perhaps in an overly simple, but helpful, way) by neuroscientist Paul MacLean as the reptilian brain and limbic system. So, we experience attraction a lot like lower animals do. The advanced parts of our brain don't really have much of a say. The neocortex (the name given to the advanced system of brain centers) can *override* feelings of attraction, so we don't act on them, but attraction isn't seated there.

If you don't believe me, then ask yourself this question: why is it you are attracted to the hot, mean, and reckless blonde you met at the club, but not the sweet and smart obese girl who has a crush on you at work? It is because attraction isn't logical. Logic says you should date a nice, smart, and stable girl. Your limbic and reptilian brains, shaped by many years of evolution, tell you a hot blonde girl is more likely to be fertile and produce healthy offspring. Unfortunately, the clunky nature of evolution has made it so our one "brain" is more like three brains of varying evolutionary ages that often don't see eye-to-eye.

Also, the emotion centers in a woman's brain are larger and more active than in a guy's, so she is more likely to make decisions based on emotion, rather than logic. This may seem sexist, but studies show women are more "emotionally intelligent" than men, and any fifth-grader can tell you girls cry a lot more than guys do at movies, big events, etc. (see "Introduction" in The Female Brain by Brizendine).

So, when women sit down and make a "list" of traits they look for in a guy, it is their neocortex working. It makes sense. It is logical. However, as science and any woman will tell you, falling in love is much messier and emotional than this.

Let me give you another example. How many women do you know who have dated an asshole at some point in their lives? If your answer is "all of them," then you are correct. Now, tell me how many women have ever put "asshole" on the list of traits they look for in a man? If you said "none," you are correct again.

My point is that when a woman says she wants a tall guy, this is simply her logical brain at work in an emotionally neutral moment. If you follow the advice in this book, you can easily get her limbic system to ponder your potential attractiveness.

Have you ever seen a hot woman with a short guy and thought to yourself, "How did *he* get *her*?" You are probably right that before he met her, she probably told her friends that her "Mr. Right" was a tall guy. She may have even told the short guy that at some point before they dated! However, that short guy followed a simple tip we teach our clients: *don't believe what a woman says; observe her behavior instead.*

Women and men are notoriously bad about knowing what they want in life. A guy may say he is happy in a job, yet take the next good offer that comes his way because deep-down he hates it. Women often claim to want something in a relationship and tell everybody about it, and then do the opposite. She may say she wants a "sweet" guy and then date only jerks.

So, instead of taking her logical attraction preferences at face value, be your best and most-confident self and see what happens with her. Maybe her "list" has "he must be over six-foot tall," but she has actually dated guys much shorter in the past. Maybe her list has "he must make six-figures," but she was engaged for two years to a guy who worked at Burger King. *Never* let a woman's preferences, rooted in pure logic, stop you from trying (if you are interested).

Also, it is important to realize that ideal preferences are different from reality. Most guys dream of playing professional sports or designing video games for a living. Instead, they end up being reasonably happy teaching high school and playing some pick-up basketball on Sundays.

Let's look at your average guy's romantic preferences too. When asked, he would probably prefer dating a hot, thin, girl with a beautiful face, like Megan Fox. Reality is much different, and guys end up dating women that look a lot less ideal than Megan. When women say they want a tall guy, it is akin to you wanting a girl like Megan Fox. Most women and men end up settling far below the ideal goals they put down on paper. So, never let a woman's ideal fantasy stop you from engaging her romantically.

I should note that from an evolutionary standpoint women can be much choosier than men. This is why most men would pretty much date any woman who looks reasonably pretty, but women will not. Biologically, having a child takes up far more of a woman's resources than producing a child does for a guy. Ethics and tribal commitments aside, a man can impregnate and leave. A woman biologically commits to nine months of pregnancy, and the child-rearing that follows (see Evolutionary Psychology: A Critical Introduction).

Thus, a woman has a lot more to lose from choosing a bad sexual partner, which is why evolution has made women much pickier than men. Nonetheless, if you are attractive, despite their choosiness, women will choose you over others.

This chapter may make some people uncomfortable. Is it manipulating women to not listen to their attraction preferences? First, let me say that when a woman says, "No!" to any physical advance, take it as an actual "no." I don't condone rape or sexual assault. Second, it is not manipulation to be your most attractive self, thereby appealing to a woman's limbic system. Being attractive is a good thing, not a bad thing. Finally, there is nothing wrong with being smart about dating. The short guys that get hot women observe instead of listen.

Your assignment is to understand that attraction is much messier than anything that can be contained on a list, and to start taking her list-based approach to dating with a grain of salt. Maybe she really does only date tall guys who make six-figures with brunette hair and green eyes. Or…maybe reality is much different, and that reality could be dating you.

Chapter Twenty-Three

The (Dreaded) Friend Zone

When I was in seventh grade, I was at a dance with a good friend of mine. Dan was a cool guy who was pretty successful with women. We were both staring at Leah, an eighth grader, from across the gym. Dan liked her, but already had a girlfriend. He told me I should ask her to dance. I told him I couldn't because I knew her when she was five. And, even though we hadn't spoken in nine years, I didn't want to ruin our childhood friendship!

Dan burst out laughing (you might be as well, which is okay) and called it what it was: a lame excuse. But, it was a defense mechanism. Tired of being friend-zoned as a preteen, I coped by putting myself there at the start. I guess you could call it "preemptive friend-zoning."

That's how intimately familiar I was with that horrible place where the romantic dreams of men go to die.

There's nothing wrong with female friends. I have many and value them. The problem occurs when you want more from a woman, but only end up as a friend. Friend-zoning almost always results from a failed dating strategy.

Some guys think that being a girl's friend will get them romantic action down the line. If they only do enough to make her a good friend, then eventually she'll fall in love with them and be the perfect girlfriend. However, it rarely works out this way. Women, believe it or not, actually see the guy as a…wait for it…friend! They're just as shocked when a guy announces his desire for romance as you would be if your best guy-friend told you he had a crush on you.

This is because women, like men, typically separate people into attracted vs. non-attracted categories. You might have a friendship with a sweet little old lady down the street. I doubt that you'll ever want to date her, no matter how deep your friendship becomes.

The same is true of your female friends. Unless they see you as attractive, you can be their best friend in the world and they won't want more (and will be genuinely shocked when you suggest it).

That's why the key to avoiding the friend-zone (or escaping it) is to get her to find you attractive. In other words, she has to think, "I want to date this guy" rather than, "Aww, he'd be a great friend." Even if she doesn't see you as immediately dateable, she at least has to see that as a possibility. If you get in the friend-zone, odds are you're going to stay there.

All of the tips below assume you know how to build at least some rapport with a woman (Chapter 31). If she doesn't feel an emotional connection with you, romance won't happen. Keep this in mind.

The first way to stay out of the friend-zone is to be high-value and attractive. That's really not a technique, but even if you try the other tips below, this one is essential. Basically, by being a confident, high-value male (and showing it), you're going to instantly push those attraction buttons. At that point, if you properly execute the next advice, it's pretty easy to get her to like you.

Second, you have to always be closing, and be bold about it, which means keeping the end in mind. What is that end? Sex? A relationship? If so, make all your choices with your goal in mind. People who succeed in every endeavor always keep the goal in mind, whether it's in business or their social lives. So, every step of the way, remember that you want to be with this woman romantically, not as a friend.

This may seem non-genuine or too focused. However, remember that if you don't want friendship, then why pursue that route? Most guys who befriend a girl don't really want friendship; they are going through the motions of being her friend in hopes of getting more. When they don't get anything more, most guys cut off the "friendship" anyway, and become bitter and angry toward the girl. So, why even bother to go down that route if it will just lead to misery? Instead, keep what you want in mind the whole time: romance.

Third, you have to stand up to the girl you like. Most guys believe that agreeing with a woman (even when they don't) will make them boyfriend material. Girls say they want a sensitive guy who will listen all the time, but examine whom they actually date. Odds are he doesn't fit that description. He likely stands up to her and tells her what he feels. Trust me, if she is emotionally unloading to you about her jerk boyfriend, you will never be her boyfriend.

You don't have to be rude, just indicate when you disagree. For example, if she starts to emotionally unload on you about her bad-boy boyfriend, then say something like, "Yeah, I've heard enough about him for this decade. We can discuss something else for now and continue that discussion in 2024." If she says how much she loves Dave Matthews, tell her you think he sucks. You can think of your own additional responses.

It may be mentally painful to disagree with her because it still might seem rude. But, get over that way of thinking. If you've been friend-zoned multiple times over the years, you still might automatically do the same things that got you there to begin with. Try something new. Be disagreeable. You have my permission and encouragement.

If you actually do agree with her on a topic, or don't mind hearing her mean boyfriend stories, then by all means, give her your time.

However, never agree to do something with the intention of kissing up. That won't make you her boyfriend.

Fourth, you have to be bold and escalate the relationship romantically. Just going with the flow and acting like a friend either puts you in the friend-zone or gets you outright rejected. Escalation means you're taking the relationship from friendly (notice not "friend"), which is the first step, to sexual. This is done in a few ways.

You have to flirt. By flirting you're telling her that you are interested in her beyond friendship. Flirting if you're a guy is typically tied to teasing (see Chapter 12). So, tease her and be playful from the very start. Having a deep philosophical conversation and discussing common interests is good. But, even friends do that. Throw in the flirting to show you're more than just a friend.

You also have to create sexual tension. This is when you feel that slight unease (and excitement) of knowing that there's a romantic spark present. Sexual tension often comes through flirting combined with a sense of attraction felt by both parties.

Women are much more passive in relationships so you'll have to take the lead. That's actually good news because you can lead her into greater attraction to you! So, you have to create that sexual tension and set a romantic tone.

The best way to do this is to add sexual escalators into the mix often. These are verbal or body language indicators that you are interested in her beyond friendship. I recommend throwing at least two or three of them in every longer interaction. So, if you meet her and talk for fifteen minutes, throw out a few. When you follow up texting later, add a few escalators to that.

While every conversation shouldn't be overtly sexual, those escalators ensure you don't drift into the friend-zone. Avoid escalators in professional or other inappropriate environments. Also avoid using them during the first interaction unless you are sure of attraction or want to push the envelope a little.

Some examples of sexual escalators are:

Verbal

- Yeah I'm great on the basketball court…Oh you mean playing basketball? I'm good at that too.

- I don't bite…well, unless you want me to.

Body Language

- Putting your arms around her waist.

- Touching her lips with your fingers.

Make sure you always pick escalators that are confident and dominant. This isn't about sappy sweet talk. The goal isn't to raise her self-esteem. It's to get her thinking of you as her boyfriend. Notice how all of the above aren't just compliments (or even compliments at all). They're putting ideas in her head about you and her.

Are they bold? Yes. But, remember the second piece of advice. Your goal is to make her attracted to you and I assume get what comes with romance (i.e. "making out" bare minimum). That is your end, so your conversation needs to move beyond casual discussion to that end. You're not talking only about sex, but you're putting it into the conversation because that is ultimately what you want!

Obviously, know when to use these escalators. It is important you keep her safety and security in mind. Limit sexual escalators until you're sure she wants to receive them, and you have built some genuine rapport (Chapter 31). Otherwise, they may come across as creepy. Be appropriate and use humor to deliver them, if possible. For example, never deliver the lines mentioned above in a way that is so straightforward that you might scare her off. Doing it all with humor and charm will put her at ease but also keep the tension alive.

You might be nervous injecting escalators into the conversation. However, if you don't escalate, then you'll just settle into being her friend. And, if she rejects you based on your escalation? Well, that brings us to the final tip, which is...

Be bold. You have seen that word a lot in this chapter because it is the key to not being friend-zoned. You have to make it clear what you want, and this ultimately means not worrying about rejection and losing her as a "friend." Being rejected is a part of life. You will be rejected. Being friend-zoned is ultimately rejection, except the process is drawn out. If you follow these tips and she still rejects you, then big deal! You've just saved months of trying to be her "friend" only to be rejected down the line. You can start fresh and move on to another girl.

And, I should note many women value confidence so much, that even if they reject your advances, they may still be so impressed they will still want to be your acquaintance. I knew a guy who constantly escalated with a girl who wasn't interested. During a conversation he escalated, and she told him, "You know I won't date you!" and then they went back to their friendly interaction.

Of course, you might be thinking these tips are primarily geared towards guys *avoiding* the friend-zone and that's true. *Escaping* the friend-zone is a lot tougher.

Why? Because if you've known the girl for a long time, then you have already established yourself as just a friend. Being her lover now would be like your best buddy from high school suddenly declaring his love for you!

Of course, unless you are secretly gay that would be very awkward. If you don't play your cards right it'll be just as awkward if you try it with a long time female friend!

If you want to leave the friend-zone, you'll have to follow the previous tips and let her gradually see the new you emerging.

Let her see you becoming more high-value. Hopefully it's becoming more obvious to everyone (if you're following the advice and practicing). It should be to her as well. If not, make it clear over time.

This will lay the foundation for her to see you as more attractive and more appropriate for dating.

Also, start thinking and acting with the end in mind. If your new goal is romance, then you'll have to shift into that mode. Stop doing friend type activities with her and move it more in a romantic direction. Obviously, that requires escalation.

Tread slowly here with your current female friends. She's known you as a friend for a while. You need to gradually shift her focus. If you move forward too quickly, she'll likely think you're creepy or that you're just going through a phase. You need to escalate gradually. Throw out a few examples of escalation here and there at the start. Then, add more. Feel out where it's all going.

Also, because of the current friendship frame you have with a girl, you might want to try to give her less of your time if you want to move to romance. That way, you can present to her the new, improved attractive you after an absence. It'll make your transformation more obvious and possibly even get that attraction spark going in a new way.

One thing you have to realize if you want to try to be romantic with a current friend is that, in this case, you genuinely might lose her as friend. Or, at the very least it could become awkward. So, you'll have to decide if you want to keep the friendship. Remember, there are a lot of fish in the sea, so if this is a genuine friendship, is it really worth it?

So, you don't have to be put in the friend-zone. Or, like I did, preemptively friend-zone yourself! You can choose to have female friends, or you can choose to pursue romance and let the chips fall, with either romance or rejection.

For this chapter, I'd like you to make a list of all the girls who've friend-zoned you in the past or are currently doing so. If you can't remember all of them, don't worry. Just list a few. Analyze, using the previous advice, where you went wrong (e.g. you didn't escalate, weren't high-value, didn't stand up to her, etc.). Then, list ways you could've avoided the friend-zone in those particular situations. This exercise will help you avoid taking a trip to the friend zone in the future.

Chapter Twenty-Four

Types, Not Leagues

When I was in college, a good friend of mine explained to me an interesting dating philosophy. He told me how he tended to pick "back of the pack" types of girls. He was speaking in evolutionary language. He liked the ones whom no one else did. They weren't very pretty and had serious issues. But, for him (yes, he was short), they were easier pickings. He always had girlfriends, but they weren't really all that satisfying to him (as he would later admit).

He either felt that he wasn't capable of dating beautiful women or couldn't be bothered with the effort they required. He thought that decent girls were clearly "out of his league." Lots of guys think in terms of this philosophy. And, it's ridiculous. Let me explain why.

You can look at other people in two primary ways. The first is the "leagues" view that my friend believed: people are categorized into levels, from easily obtainable to "out of my league." This view creates a pecking order and implies that beautiful girls are somehow radically different from men. We put them on a pedestal and consider ourselves unworthy to associate with them. Remember, putting women on pedestals is bad.

The second view sees others in terms of "types." People can be in preferred or non-preferred categories (e.g. preppy, hipster, ditzy blonde, etc.) and you may prefer one to another for dating. But, with the types perspective, no girl is off limits simply because she is too beautiful or too anything. This is how successful daters view the world.

By thinking in terms of leagues, you are limiting your chances at success with women. Looking at girls in terms of types is different. It makes you in charge of your destiny. No girl is above you in any way. You may strike out with girls, but by not putting a girl into a "league," you don't self-select yourself out of a possible relationship with anyone.

Of course, I also want you to be realistic, at least of your evaluation of yourself. If you are going after the most beautiful women in a club, are you on the same level? If she's drop-dead gorgeous, but you're lacking in confidence and value, then why would she want to date you? However, if you are truly confident, successful, and high-value, then, yes, you can date anyone, no matter your height.

When I was in my darkest, least-confident days, I still noticed a lot of ugly dudes with hot women. They were just confident and bold enough to win over females. And, it started with not limiting themselves with "league thinking."

However, don't use your recognition of "types" to limit yourself either. Mentally admitting that you never approach certain "types" of girls due to the challenges they present is just an excuse. A client once told me he doesn't like the hot, confident "type" of woman because they're too hard to approach and win over. That's just "league" thinking using different language!

Also, don't get so caught up in putting people into types that you close yourself off to a diverse group of girls.

Avoiding "league" thinking is another way to get women down from that proverbial pedestal most guys put them on. If you go into any relationship thinking the other person is inherently "better" than you, then you aren't going to be your best self. Getting rid of "league thinking" will also allow you to view women as normal human beings.

It's going to take a little while to get used to thinking differently about women. We are accustomed to creating a little hierarchy among ourselves. However, you know better. And the "types" way of thinking gives you access to any girl you want, whatever her position on the supposed hierarchy.

Your assignment for this chapter is to believe that there are types, not leagues. But, before you get off too easily, I want you to go out to a club, mall, or other busy venue and find a girl that, if you believed in hierarchies (and you don't), would be the most intimidating one in the place. I want you to go and talk to her. Just be friendly and strike up a conversation.

I want you to notice a couple of things. One, she really is human, just like you, and may actually be pretty cool. Two, even if she isn't interested in you, it's not the end of your world to find out that fact. You may even make a nice connection.

Also, as for my friend? He eventually started dating a former student, a drop-dead gorgeous redhead. Why? As a college professor, he had the whole power and value thing going for him. See, if you improve your confidence and value, there really are no leagues, only types.

Chapter Twenty-Five

"Shit Tests"

In college, I liked a pretty, smart girl named Terra. I pretty much put myself in the friend-zone, but in spite of my efforts to fail, I actually got a date with her (she probably asked me). We had a good time at the movies, and even shared a kiss when I dropped her off at the dorm.

Then, she unleashed a total bombshell. She said she wasn't sure if we were a good fit for each other. Even though I really liked her, I told her that I agreed with her assessment! I was a total idiot. She gave me a "shit test" and I failed miserably.

We've all had moments when we were trying to date a girl, things seemed to be going well, and she unexpectedly threw a statement out of left field. Or, maybe, a better baseball image is a curveball. We think she likes us, all is going well, then…BOOM! She makes a comment or asks a question that seems to indicate she's no longer interested, even though the previous evidence says otherwise.

These comments, which usually come out of the blue, are commonly called "shit tests." They are conversational traps, designed to test your value as a man. Yes, these are like those pop quizzes with trick questions you had in high school. Except these are designed to test what kind of a man you are. Hint: the goal is to show her you're a real one.

Are these tests fair? Probably no more fair than the science pop quiz you failed in high school because you were unprepared. But, life isn't fair. And, women will throw out these tests frequently. It's an evolutionary defense mechanism. They want to make sure you're a high-value man worthy of their limited supply of eggs. And it is likely subconscious. Women probably aren't consciously testing you, but that doesn't mean they aren't doing it.

It's worth mentioning that women throw out shit tests to all guys: tall, short, fat, skinny, high-value, and low-value. However, short guys often face more shit testing than others. It's because when we are short our value is automatically questioned. And, when it comes to testing short men, it almost always becomes about our height.

Just as the nerd who studied every night passed the pop quiz you failed, now you'll have the knowledge to pass these shit tests. Here are a few general tips. We've also included, as bonus material in

"Appendix B," some great responses to shit tests, especially if you're short.

Generally, shit tests are ways she disqualifies you from dating her (or her disqualifying herself). She is determining if you're worth her attention.

The most common shit tests she might throw out are mentioning a guy who likes her (or boyfriend), an inability to date (religious reasons, busy, etc.), a flaw in your personality, etc. Shit tests are usually offhand comments randomly inserted into the conversation.

Keep in mind that these tests aren't insults and they don't mean the girl isn't attracted to you. To the contrary, if she is showing you other signs of attraction, then it likely means she is attracted to you, at least tentatively. How you respond determines her level of attractiveness to you and if she's going to proceed with you romantically.

First, you'll have to identify what is a shit test and what is just her stating the facts. Sometimes, it's unclear. Obviously there are girls who aren't attracted to you and genuinely might want you just to go away and leave them alone.

If her body language and words tell you that she's attracted to you, and she gives you crap, then you're likely dealing with a shit test. If her mannerisms and words tell you that she doesn't like you, then her efforts to disqualify you are probably indicative of her lack of attraction. That's okay. There are plenty of fish in the sea. Just make sure to read the situation correctly.

Once you've determined that you're being tested, you'll have to pass. Passing means you show yourself to be high-value enough to date her. That's right. She's questioning if you're actually worth dating. You have to make that answer a resounding "yes." Here's how.

The first and most important rule when experiencing a shit test is to remain cool and relaxed. Shit tests are meant to rattle your confidence and throw you off of your game. Remember, she's looking for a confident guy. If a comment makes you angry, anxious, or rattled, you're failing.

So, even if she throws out a ridiculously stupid or insensitive comment, you cannot appear upset. That means you can't look disappointed, sad, angry, or jealous. Act like her comment means absolutely nothing to you. Definitely, don't argue with her about any issue. You will lose every pissing contest with women. They're not going to give in.

Let me give you an example. I once read a story of a girl who told a group of her colleagues she thought a particular actor would have been attractive, if he weren't so short. While that statement was not a shit test per se, a short guy in the group got offended by the comment. He proceeded to argue with her about the heightism, discrimination, etc., inherent in her statement. The girl, feeling backed into a corner over a comment she probably just made off-hand, defended herself verbally and refused to give in. By the end of the conversation, the girl remarked that she had "clearly touched a nerve" with the short guy.

The short guy in question proclaimed how proud he was of himself for standing up for short people. Unfortunately, he did a lot more harm than good. Had he responded correctly (as we describe here), he'd be known at work as "that confident and funny guy." However, he is now probably known as "that guy who is really sensitive about his height." By getting worked up, he showed he cared.

Let me give you another example. If she mentions another guy she's dating, don't get sad or jealous. Definitely don't lecture her about leading you on or wasting your time. She might not even be dating another guy! In this case, the best response is to dismiss her disqualification in a clever way. Say something like, "Oh that's nice. I date lots of women myself" and move on in the conversation.

Second, you want to handle a shit test in a confident way that makes you look high-value. Notice in the previous example how the response indicates you have lots of dates too. It makes you look very attractive and popular. Even if you don't have lots of dates, say it anyway. She likely isn't dating anyone serious either. You don't want to make crazy lies (like "I have a Ferrari at home"), but she can't check up on your dating status anyway. She's giving shit; give a little back.

Finally, you'll want to respond to shit tests with a humorous wit. This is key for two reasons. First, laughing it off shows it doesn't bother you. Second, being witty is very high-value. That's why we include examples in the bonus material. And, they're almost all zingers.

Your assignment for this chapter is to read the bonus section and memorize most of the shit test answers. I'd also advise you practice saying them, even if it's just you and a friend rattling them off to each other. Next, come up with a few of your own. Maybe you have a big nose and might hear about it. Develop some witty answers to shit tests you might experience.

While I might not still be in a relationship with Terra today, at the very least I could've passed her shit test and gotten into a deeper relationship with her at the time. Emotionally freezing like a deer in headlights and agreeing with her was about the stupidest thing I could've done! You need to learn from my mistakes and pass those tests!

Chapter Twenty-Six

The Sober Truth

Earlier, I referenced a story about a rich man who was an acquaintance of a friend. The rich guy was pretty good looking, but painfully shy. The only time he could even talk to women was when he drank. He wasn't an alcoholic, but still used alcohol as a crutch when he went out or threw lavish parties at his home.

The alcohol removed a few of his inhibitions and he was able to talk to girls after several shots of whiskey. However, he would slur his speech, stumble around, and even break down and cry around the beautiful women he wanted to date. He had almost no success with women in spite of his wealth.

This scenario isn't unique to this particular guy. Many men have such few social skills and are so shy that they rely on "liquid courage" to plod their way through the dating game. This can particularly be the case for guys who have experienced a lot of rejection or had little success with women (like many short men). And, these guys often have similar results as the friend of my friend.

Throughout the book, I've mentioned bars and clubs a lot. I'm honestly not a huge fan of these places for meeting new people. Most men and women at bars are trying to project an image of who they want to be, not who they really are. And everyone knows it. So, everyone's guard is up. In addition, lots of girls are drunk, so it can be hard to start a meaningful relationship if that's what you want.

At many clubs, you find desperate guys making fools of themselves and hitting on girls who want nothing to do with them. But, you can't blame the women either. They want quality men, but then have to sort through fifteen drunk losers with bad pickup lines just to maybe find one outstanding guy (and, even then, still don't).

In spite of my issues with these establishments, you'll find that my discussion throughout the next few chapters assumes that you'll be picking up girls at a club. I do this because, like it or not, these locations are where a lot of people end up on a Friday or Saturday night.

You don't have to do this and if you don't, then good for you. But, I'm not going to fight the culture on this; I realize that a lot of guys will be trying these techniques in clubs. That's cool, but I do want you to be aware of a few things.

First, these environments are typically high stress. While that's not ideal in some ways, it can be in another way. Busy clubs and bars can be good "practice." If you can handle the environment of a singles club, then you can approach and close anywhere. Having trained under the most stressful and negative conditions, when you meet people in your everyday life, the techniques you've learned in this book will be much easier to execute.

Second, it's important to develop a social life outside of those settings. Hanging out at a bar, especially if you have a reason for being there (watching sports, eating dinner, meeting new people, or dancing) is acceptable, but being the guy who never leaves is very low value. If you just like to drink a lot, you might need to evaluate why putting a liquid in your body is so important to you.

Society is fickle in this regard. It promotes drinking at every turn (just watch all the beer commercials), but judges drunks very harshly. You don't want to be "that guy" known around town for hanging out in a bar all day. Make sure you diversify your environments, not only for social practice, but also to be a healthy, well-rounded person. Visit coffee shops, festivals, religious or civic events, work functions, etc. Being an attractive guy means being popular in a variety of places anyway.

Third, bars and clubs are often very loud and chaotic. A lot of the techniques in this book center on showing your high value and winning girls through humor, language manipulation techniques, and building rapport. It's really tough to do that if you can't even hear the person next to you. In fact, if a place is too loud, women will fall back on the sense they can use: their sight. Then, your shortness becomes a disadvantage again.

If you do start at a loud bar and manage to meet someone nice and open, try to move to a different place, like a restaurant or coffee shop where you can actually talk to the person. Then, you can show her how even more awesome you are.

Finally, if you do go out to bars and clubs, stay sober when picking up females. This is for a couple of reasons. Number one, you need to learn and master these techniques and internalize them without a chemical crutch.

For example, approaching strangers can be tough, but it's something you need to do without the help of liquid courage. Number two, at those places most people are either drunk or at least slightly impaired. If you have your wits, you will be far more successful since you start with an immediate advantage.

If you think you have a problem with drugs or alcohol, don't suffer in silence. You're not alone. Addiction is a disease, meaning that it is something that needs treatment, just like diabetes or a broken bone. Find a community substance abuse agency or an Alcoholics Anonymous meeting in your area and get some help.

Your practice for this chapter is to write down a list of venues where you can go out and meet new people. Be specific, writing down their actual names, and include at least three that are not clubs or bars. If you can't think of any venues or any non-bar places, then do some research. Find a place that looks like it would be busy, fun, and match your values. This will help you for the next chapters, which involve going out and actually approaching women.

Chapter Twenty-Seven

The Inevitability Of Rejection

I was in fourth grade and Devon was just about the hottest thing my nine year old mind could fathom. I liked her and made an effort to get to know her in the hopes that I could "get her to be my girlfriend." However, she had her sights set on Bernie, who was much taller than I was (both then and now). She and Bernie became "boyfriend and girlfriend."

But, something remarkable happened. A month later, Bernie broke up with Devon and I asked her out. She said "yes." I was in heaven. She was my first "girlfriend" and I was ready to do all that fourth grade girlfriend stuff like hold hands and swing together.

Alas, it wasn't meant to be. Women, even at eight (she was in third grade) could be very manipulative. She only dated me to get back at Bernie. And, it worked. Within a week, I was dumped so she could be with the tall man of her dreams.

Let's just say I didn't take the rejection well. I think I went through each stage of grief and then some. I remember crying and being angry at Devon. But, above all, I remember being frustrated that I had no control over being rejected.

Rejection hurts. We have evolved to pair up, both for sex and emotional comfort. And, this is an incredible need that is hard-wired into our brains. Yet, it's a need that we absolutely cannot meet without another person consenting. Rejection by a woman stings because it keeps us from achieving what we are literally designed to do: procreate.

As a result, rejection by women hurts much more than just about any other form of rejection. Even such important things as getting cut from teams or not getting a job pale in comparison to the emotional damage typically wrought from not getting that "yes" from a woman.

Ben Franklin said, "The only certain thing in life is death and taxes." Since Ben was a bit of a player himself, I'm surprised he didn't add "and romantic rejection" to his quote since if you are in the dating game, then rejection isn't simply a possibility or a probability. Being rejected is an absolute certainty. Granted some guys avoid rejection by refusing to try. But, that doesn't count. If you seek women, you'll be rejected. A lot. Period.

However, rejection isn't the end of the world. If you're going to successfully date and get into a long term relationship, you'll have to learn how to handle rejection. Here is my best advice for getting over the pain of rejection.

First, you'll have to make rejection seem "normal." I know this tip sounds odd, but bear with me. I drink a lot of coffee. I spill some of it quite often. However, spilling a little bit of coffee for most people is "normal." I don't flip out, cry, or stop drinking coffee. I accept it as a part of drinking my favorite drink and deal with it when it arises. I wipe it up and move on.

If you are going to successfully date women, then rejection has to become normal. You get rejected, you pick yourself back up, and you move on. If you truly internalize the "rejection is normal" mantra, then you don't even have to pick yourself back up. You don't fall apart to begin with.

Second, you have to take the attitude of "no failure, just feedback." This means that you learn from your mistakes. So, if you approach a hot girl and she rejects you, then you don't see it as a failure. You see it as a great chance to become better at picking up women.

Don't overanalyze it, but think about ways you could've done better with her. Maybe you appeared nervous or tripped over your words. Perhaps you let yourself get all starry eyed over her because she was hot. Whatever the problem, see where you made miscues, then you vow not to make those mistakes again.

Third, don't take everything personally. There will be times when you won't even come up with feedback because you might have done everything right. You might have been rejected for reasons outside of your control. Maybe she has a boyfriend or doesn't want one right now (and it's not just an excuse).

Or, she might just not be attracted to you and part of it might be your height. That's okay. You can't force someone to be attracted to you. Even if you do everything right, you just might not be right for her. There are many girls who aren't right for you either. Don't take it to heart. There are people out there who are right for you. You don't want to waste your time with the ones who aren't.

Fourth, don't get mad when you're rejected. No woman "owes" you a date any more than you "owe" a woman a date. If a woman you don't find attractive approached you and you said "no," that's your choice. You can't get angry because a woman doesn't find you attractive enough to give you her number or whatever you want from her.

Fifth, don't whine or beg a woman to reconsider. Women are naturally more sympathetic than men. But, they can be hard-asses when it comes to guys who beg or whine. They'll just think you're pathetic and maybe even get one of their guy friends (or a bouncer) to get you out of their face.

While getting angry at least shows you have a slight backbone, whining or begging just makes you look totally pathetic. She'll just see you as a great big loser. And, if you are around her friends, your friends, or in a public place, everyone else will think you're a pathetic loser too. If she hurts your feelings, grow up and be a man. Don't ever beg or whine. No woman is worth losing your dignity. Vent to your guy friends later if you have to get the frustration off of your chest.

Sixth, don't argue with or rationally explain why you shouldn't be rejected to a woman. This kind of goes along with the anger advice, but is different. A guy at one of my talks approached me asking for help getting out of the friend-zone with a girl. I read some of his texts to her. Even though he had taken her out to an expensive meal (over a hundred dollars!) and she gave him a little kiss after that, she texted him that while he was a kind and generous gentleman, she wasn't interested.

He decided to rationally argue that she was really looking to date a generous and kind guy (i.e. him), because she had confided in him previously that she hated her ex-boyfriend because he lacked those traits. Logically he "had" her, right? But attraction isn't a logical, frontal-lobe matter. It meant nothing to her.

Don't argue with a woman if she rejects you. Don't explain how you're really awesome or, if she mentions your height, that she's a heightism bigot. Maybe she is. But, arguing about it in the heat of a rejection will just make you look like an angry, bitter, begging short man. Even if you simply keep it logical, with little emotion, it will still make you look extremely low-value. And, guess what? Your rant isn't going to do a damn thing to reduce discrimination either.

So, what do you do when you're rejected? I have some advice for that too. However, make sure to distinguish between a shit test and true rejection before you accept that she's not interested in you.

First, be cool and relaxed about it. Don't appear rattled in your words or body language. You might even say, "Hey, that's cool. Good luck in finding someone." This shows that you are cool and gracious. You're not kissing up, but generally wishing her the best. Guys with options can do that. They don't have any need to argue with women.

Second, you can be witty and even a little biting. If you choose this option, you have to deliver your humor in a carefree and relaxed way. If your comments come across as sarcastic or passive-aggressive, then you just appear like a needy loser. But, if you can be funny, you'll look high value and confident. Throw out one liners related to her mode of rejection. Use this only on women who aren't very nice in their rejections.

For example, if she says, "I'm not looking for a boyfriend right now" you can respond with, "Oh, so you're just about random hookups? Fine with me." If she says, "I don't date short guys," you can point to a tall, fat, and disheveled guy and say, "That guy might be more of your speed then." These comments put you at the top of the dating game, even if you're being rejected. Again, smile and joke, not be mean and passive-aggressive. If you have options, and you should, you can be funny and aloof.

Third, turn rejection into a game. When going out with buddies, for your first few approaches, *try* to get rejected. It sounds odd, but it works on a couple of levels. First, getting rejected actually becomes associated in your mind with succeeding, because he who gets rejected the most wins. Second, it turns rejection into something fun.

David and I have done this before and it really is fun. We try to be outrageous and see how badly we can get rejected. Then we have a good laugh. Getting rejected starts to lose its sting. In addition, lots of women love when we do the rejection game. Our outrageous behavior doesn't even always get us rejected because women love confident, unique guys who differ from the norm.

Finally, you can turn the tables and make it like you're actually rejecting her. This is always fun. If she says you're too short, you can say, "You're actually right about us. It won't work. I usually date girls younger than you." If she tells you she's not interested, you can say, "Yeah, we probably wouldn't work out. You're not really my speed. I need someone a tad more exciting."

By turning the tables, you are making her feel rejected and on the defensive. Even though she's rejected you, you've now come out on top. She'll be insecure as to why you didn't react in the typical way (disappointment, sadness, anger, etc.). She might even reevaluate you as she tries to uncover the reasons why you rejected her after she rejected you!

Let me address a common fear many of our clients have with what I am saying here. They are uncomfortable viewing interaction with women as a power struggle. Gentlemen, you have to realize that dating is a game; women, especially attractive ones, play it very well. Many guys don't, and the results are emotionally damaging to dudes.

I know of no football player, video gamer, etc., who would allow an opponent to totally beat up on him without at least resisting in some capacity. Coming out "on top" in the dating game doesn't mean you are a jerk or even mean; it means that you have confidently stood up for yourself and your dignity.

I should add that if you absolutely feel the need to vent or get mad about a particular rejection, save it for your guy friends or, better yet, your therapist. The most important point is not to express it when you're out in public.

I experienced rejection after rejection in elementary and middle school, to the point where I didn't even approach girls in high school, college, and graduate school. But, employing the principles in this book, I started finding more success with women later in my life. It took a while to get rid of my automatic thoughts about rejection that I had developed when I was younger. But, I did it. These tips should help you do the same.

For your assignment, I want you to identify how you feel after rejection (e.g. angry, sad, argumentative, etc.). List ways you can avoid acting this way when you're out in public trying to meet women.

Come up with some witty and high-value rejection responses, as well. Make them charming and confident, to show that you aren't bothered at all by rejection. Practice them so they sound natural when you deliver them in public.

Chapter Twenty-Eight

The Approach

The first day of my sophomore year at Ohio University, during the break between American History and Political Science class, I sat down to have a cup of coffee at my favorite coffee shop. A beautiful blonde girl sat down at a table across the room. We must've had a similar class schedule, because I saw her every single day throughout the rest of the quarter.

And, every single day I stared at her from across the coffee shop. She never entered with a guy and usually just sat down, drank some coffee, and read. I wanted to talk to her and a few times I swore I would. I once even walked over and was ready to talk. But, I clammed up. Something in me made it impossible.

Sadly, the quarter ended without me ever doing a damn thing. I saw her around campus on occasion afterwards, but the moment was gone. I couldn't man up. Even though I love my life, I still regret never approaching her.

I'm sure many readers (if not all) can relate to this story. It's not just because it's "one that got away." My pathetic story is about women who never even had a chance to get away because the guy in question never even tried.

Before we give tips to approach women, we first need to address why approaching women can be so freaking hard. Because let's face it, I really, really wanted to talk to that beautiful girl having coffee ten feet from me every single day for ten weeks. But, there was something within me that just wouldn't let me

Long ago in the history of humanity, the tribe's chief and his relatives typically pursued the best women. They also picked the best and strongest men to be their peers and warriors. These were the alpha males. The lesser men, the betas, were frequently given the leftovers (if that). If a guy was strong and powerful, he could compete. Otherwise, he was pretty much relegated to loneliness or the "back of the pack."

If a guy approached a female, there was a good chance she was taken by one of the powerful males, either as a wife or daughter. He could possibly either be killed or harmed by the woman's relatives simply for approaching her. This is true even in some Middle Eastern cultures today. This also occurs in other primate colonies: the alpha male gets most of the females, and the beta male primates only get action if they sneak behind the back of the head ape, chimp, etc.

Today, at least in the United States, it's very unlikely that you will be killed for approaching a woman at a bar. But, it does happen, especially if her husband is around the corner. Your brain has one goal for you: survival. So your evolved brain wiring tells you that if you approach a girl and fail, you very well might get physically hurt or even die. The prettier the girl, the more anxiety, because the prettiest girls are the most likely to be taken (and thus your potential to fight goes up).

You don't believe me? Think of the most beautiful girl you've ever seen. Now, think about asking her out. How do you feel? If you're a typical male, you probably feel at least a little nervous, if not scared out of your mind.

Your feeling is totally normal. It's called "approach-anxiety" and it's hard-wired into the less-developed parts of the male brain. Your more-developed brain (the "neocortex") likes a girl and wants you to ask her out, but your caveman brain (the limbic system or "Paleomammalian complex") butts in with approach-anxiety. For most guys, the older parts of the brain win in spite of your newer parts' fruitless attempts at reason.

I haven't yet met any man who has gotten rid of approach-anxiety completely, by which I mean the initial feeling he gets when thinking of approaching a woman. However, approach-anxiety can be controlled.

The first way to combat approach-anxiety is to remember that approaching someone won't kill you. You're not going to undo hundreds of thousands of years of evolution in a week, but the rational side of your brain can keep the older parts in check. Each time you are ready to approach a woman, take charge of your brain.

Acknowledge that the more primitive part of your brain is trying to sabotage you, and then remind yourself that you will not die or even likely be harmed. There is no death by rejection. Your rational side took hundreds of thousands of years to evolve, so take advantage of it! Of course, if the woman is beside a tough-looking guy who could kick your butt, listen to your limbic system.

The second method to reduce anxiety is to have a "shoot down set." This technique is for picking up women in a club or other social setting, but is probably a little much for lower-key settings. As soon as you enter a club or other venue where women are looking to meet men, approach a group of girls and ask them to shoot you down (meaning insult you). Using humor is perhaps the best way to do this (say something like, "My self-esteem is just too high tonight. I really need you to shoot me down").

If they comply, you will have been put down and guess what? You survived! This method really is helpful to banish anxiety for the rest of the night. The less-rational limbic system loses its control because your rational brain knows you're still alive. You can relax.

Also, I've found that very few women will actually shoot you down. You may even make new friends or romantic partners from this activity. But, if they do shoot you down, then guess what? You asked them to! So, they still did what you told them. This is a perfect method to break the ice no matter how they respond to your command.

Third, approach-anxiety can be countered by mastering the other techniques in this book like detachment, flexibility, humor, open body language, etc. The more confident, high-value, and detached you become, the less approach-anxiety rules your life. So, keep working on mastering the other aspects of this book too.

Finally, the key to destroying approach-anxiety is to approach others often. The more you do it, the more you'll realize that approaching new people won't kill you and you'll even discover it can actually be pretty fun. Just like anything you do, from sports to using a new phone, the more often you practice it, the more natural it becomes.

When approaching women, there are a few things to keep in mind other than just banishing approach-anxiety. After all, a guy can conquer his fear of approaching and still do a lousy job at the actual approach.

First, have fun and be detached. Keep the approach about the process, not the outcome. In other words, when you approach don't go into it hoping for a date or a relationship. Don't dwell on past failures or envision her as your future wife. Make your goal to enjoy the approach and have a good time no matter what happens.

Second, approach with another guy. We address this more in the chapter that follows on being a wingman. But, it's always best, if you can, to approach with a partner. Why? It's for a couple of reasons. You won't look like a creepy loner. In fact, you'll look like you can at least have one friend. And, your wingman can make you look even better than you actually are. That's a plus too.

Third, you'll want to make every approach as high-energy as possible. Think about something special that you really enjoy. Maybe it's a concert, important event, festival, etc. In many cases you can feel the high energy involved.

At events like this, people become enthusiastic and excited. They are happy to be there and they want to be a part of the event. You should create that kind of atmosphere wherever you go. Meeting and getting to know you should be an experience, maybe not life-changing, but at least day-changing. Even if that girl had a bad day or is sitting in the dingiest bar known to man, you should make her experience of meeting you totally electrifying.

You do this by being energetic and enthusiastic. I don't mean being peppy and fake. But, let's look at it this way. Have you ever been sold a product? If you did, it's likely because the person selling it completely believed in it. I promise you that, unless the product itself is amazing and you already know it, no one buys a product off a half-assed, bored salesperson. It's so obvious when salespersons don't believe in the product or the business.

You are selling yourself when you approach women. If you really are worth her time, then you'd better believe it yourself. Otherwise, you'll never sell it to her. Be excited about who you are. Have a sense of energy and urgency (but not desperation) about your approach. Deliver your lines with emotion and confidence. Even if you don't fully believe in yourself, act like you do. And sell yourself like crazy.

If you have trouble getting worked up into a high energy level when going out, listen to some driving music, joke around with your buddies, mentally tell yourself you're the cockiest guy in town, etc. Whatever it takes, do it. We gave some body language poses (see Chapter 20) that help too. Make the evening high-energy, even if the venue or the crowd isn't. Your job is to transform the dynamic; don't let it transform you!

Fourth, keep the approach in perspective. Lots of guys put all sorts of ridiculous scenarios in their heads as they approach girls. They worry about being shot down, looking foolish, etc. I've been shot down many times and, yes, I've looked like a total jackass on occasion.

But, guess what? I can't tell you what the girl even looked like! And…guess what too? The biggest jackasses are actually the dudes quietly staring at women from afar who are too afraid to approach.

Unless you're approaching someone you've known for a while, most likely you're going up to complete strangers. Even if you do look foolish or get shot down, who cares? You likely won't see the person ever again. So, who cares what some stranger you will never see again thinks about you? We often look back on our foibles and laugh about them! Besides, if you fail too miserably, just go to another place for the night and start over.

Finally, become what our friends call us: "approach machines." Yes, we've actually been told that. We are approach machines because once we get started, we approach anybody and everybody we, or our clients, find attractive. We go from venue to venue, approaching anyone we feel like. It's fun and it's exciting. To get to this point in your dating life is amazing.

So, if you get turned down, move right along to a new group. If the conversation is becoming boring or you don't think she's going to give you her number, move right along. Approach, approach, approach. We talk about this more in Chapter 29.

I want to say a few things about pick-up lines since a lot of people ask about them. Do they work? The answer is "yes and no." Great, original pick-up lines typically work. But, not always. Here are a few pieces of advice to open up a conversation.

First, make your opening line original. Women have heard almost all of the classic ones. They're no longer funny or unique, especially with the invention of the internet. The prettiest girls will likely have heard them and just think you're another schmuck.

Second, try to use observational humor when you open up. It shows you're original and witty, both of which are high-value traits. If you establish that you're high-value with the first line, winning her over is that much easier. In addition, a high-value, original, and witty opener will also make you stand out from the rest of the losers.

Finally, remember the pick-up line is just one part of the approach. Your pick-up line should be tied into whatever routines you have planned to do or your general personality. Some guys worry so much about having the right pick-up lines that they forget that alone won't cut it. A random pick-up line thrown out with no context or follow-up will just make you look stupid.

Keep in mind that approaching girls, especially lots of them, will be hard at first. But, it's an important risk to take because the reward can be amazing: a fun time or maybe even a long term relationship.

Your assignment is to go out on a busy night to a club or other venue and approach five random people. However, let me give you a word of advice: it's best to go somewhere where people are anticipating an approach, at least if this is your first time. I'd recommend a social event, club, or busy coffee shop. If it's busier, then you're also not going to be singled out for unwanted attention.

Remember to use your routines. Try to keep the conversation going, but at this point don't stress too much about follow-up. Just approach five people. Try a "shoot down set" if you're up to it. I want you to see that approaching isn't going to kill you, and that the opposite is true: it can be fun.

Also, as the last chapter mentioned, you might want to think about making a game out of rejection at the first venue. This will help relax you for the night.

Chapter Twenty-Nine

Winging

When David and I go out to help our clients meet women, we have a distinct advantage in winning over women: we're twins! Because of that, we know each other well and are great partners. And, there's always the novelty factor of adult twins.

When we act as wingmen for our guys, they rarely get shot down. Even if our clients are hesitant or anxious, our skills make up for it. It's like how a great offensive line and amazing receivers can make an average quarterback look like a pro bowler.

This chapter is about being a wingman. For the uninitiated, a wingman is the male sidekick in a romantic approach. So, if you are approaching a group of beautiful women, your wingman is the guy who will have your back and help you (hopefully) get the girl.

Being a wingman is actually a pretty cool role. It's like the color man in sports announcing. He doesn't have to do the hard work of calling the play by play. He simply has to add his thoughts to the conversation.

The wingman has a similar role. He doesn't do the hard work of approaching. His primary goal is to make the guy approaching look valuable. And, he needs to make himself look valuable in the process.

Short guys are especially in need of good wingmen because being short automatically comes across as lower value to some girls. That means from the very start you have to work harder to win them over. It's a lot easier if you have a cool guy in your corner.

That's where an experienced wingman comes in. And, since we've done so well winging others, we'll share our tips to help you.

First, keep your role in mind. You're there to support your friend, not hog the glory. So, you let your friend lead and try not to change roles in the middle of the approach. If your friend is faltering, it's your job to help prop him up, not save the day. However, if he's completely pathetic and losing the girls, by all means take over. But, unless it's truly that bad, support him first.

This also means that you don't go for the close, get her number, or steal his thunder. If you really like the girl, then you approach and he can wing you. But, decide that in advance. If she gravitates towards you and shows no interest in him, that's fine. Go ahead and close. But, don't encroach on your friend's territory without at least tacit permission first.

Second, make sure you know a lot about the person you're winging and that you have very good rapport with him. David and I succeed because of this factor. We are like two comedians when we go out. We know each other well and can act the part with perfection. This is because we've practiced in public a lot. And, the twin bonding thing helps.

Go out and practice with your friend and you'll get better. Try some humor routines, work on teasing, playing off of each other, etc. You'll want to have great chemistry with your friend when you act as a wingman. If you aren't used to working with each other in this way, then both of you will fall flat when it comes time to pick up women.

Third, make him look good at all costs. Lots of wingmen think they're being cute or funny by poking fun at the guy they're winging. Maybe the girl will throw out a shit test and the wingman will join in teasing his friend. Never do that. Guys tease girls, not the other way around. By teasing or mocking your friend, you're lowering his value in the girl's eyes.

So, brag about your friend and build up his image with the girls. You can say something like, "We're out celebrating his recent pay raise" or "He just ran a half-marathon; I think he deserves a kiss" etc.

Hopefully the guy you're winging actually has some high-value skills and accomplishments. Let those be known. Also, draw positive attention back to your buddy as much as possible.

Finally, try to make picking up girls a group affair where everyone wins. As a wingman, you don't have to go home alone. You can approach groups of girls and then pursue your own girl within the group.

A good wingman will help his buddy, then, when his buddy is succeeding, pursue one of the girls himself. If your friend succeeded and you made him look good, then guess what? You look good too! You should have no trouble getting one of the girls in the group to like you as well. And, if he's gotten the girl, he can then make you look good in the eyes of her friends.

For your assignment, find a fun, cool single male friend and go out at some point this week and approach several groups of girls. Before you go out, develop or find some opening lines and humor routines. Practice them a few times together. Then, go out and actually try them.

Trade off between being the lead and the wingman. Try to develop some chemistry and see what works for the two of you and what doesn't. This isn't high pressure. You're going out with your buddy to have a good time and practice, and nothing more.

I want you to realize when you're doing this practice session how leading and winging are different roles. You might be better at one than the other. However, it's good to be proficient in both areas because one might come more naturally.

Also, when you go out, you'll increase your chances of both you and your friend finding success in the dating game. Don't underestimate how great an asset a wingman can be in helping you get an amazing girl to like you.

Chapter Thirty

Be Like Boomhauer

Boomhauer: Yeah, man, check it out, man. Went and entered (the phone number) in my dang ol' Palm Pilot.

Bobby Hill: But you got shot down by twenty-three women before you got that phone number!

Boomhauer: Ain't no thing.

Bobby Hill: So, this is your big secret? You just ask every woman you see until one of them finally says yes?

Boomhauer: Shh, man! You going to tell my secret, man (From the television show King of The Hill, "I'm With Cupid").

One of the themes of self-loathing short men is how disadvantaged they are in the dating game. They like to trot out statistics showing how most women will reject guys under a certain height or how only a certain percentage will even give a guy a chance if he's too short. First of all, people's theoretical standards are fluid. That's why we address online dating in this book.

However, let's look at the statistics. Let's say that seventy percent of women would never, ever, under any condition date a short man. That means a short guy is absolutely limited, without exception, to thirty percent of women. I made up both numbers and I'm sure the seventy percent number is way inflated. But, let's just assume, for argument's sake, that number is accurate.

Using my inflated numbers, that means a short guy who has basic skills with women can approach ten women and have absolutely no chance with any of them! Oh wait…He would have a real chance with three of them. He approaches twenty, which is very possible at a series of busy venues over a several hour period, and he could easily find success with six. If he went out two nights in a row, there are twelve possible women. Batting .300 is still a very respectable average.

The chapter's namesake is a character from the TV show King of the Hill. Boomhauer is a ladies man in the fictional town of Arlen, Texas. At a shoe store, he approached twenty-three women and struck out with twenty-two. But, hey, that one was all that mattered.

I love this episode because it illustrates an essential point of the dating game: you have to approach to find success. You might even have to approach a lot of women, especially if you're short and dealing with a woman's height barrier.

This is easy advice. But, it's also absolutely easier said than done. Having the guts to approach one or two women, let alone forty, over a two-day period is incredibly rare. Hell, I'm guessing there are guys reading this book that have never even approached a random woman (a "cold" approach) in their entire lives!

Still, it can be done. And, if done properly, you can go from being dateless to a freaking dating machine. But, unless you are the most outgoing person in the world, it could be tough. We're not going to discuss much about approach tips here since that was the point of the last few chapters. But, we do want to address a couple techniques to approach a lot of people in one night.

First, you have to embrace detachment (see Chapter 9) and not fear rejection (Chapter 26). Recall that detachment means not being attached to a particular outcome, but still being your best self and doing what you know to be right.

Well, if you are detached, you are going to do what you know to be right, which is approaching lots of women, even if they might reject you. You will start to enjoy approaching lots of girls because that is what the new and confident "you" does, regardless of their responses. If you have been shy or your dating experiences have been underwhelming, this is a chance to finally put talking to lots and lots of women in its proper perspective, which is that it is fun and exciting.

Second, as I mentioned previously, you can turn approaching women into a game, especially when you go out with your buddies (and you should). Pair off into groups or, if it's just a couple of you, make a bet to see who can take the lead in approaching the most women. Or, do it with both approaches and closes (phone numbers, etc.). Maybe the guy who collects the most phone numbers gets his drinks bought next time.

Do you notice how all of these tips relate to being relaxed and just having a good time? This goes back to detachment. If you can turn the process of approaching women into a blast, then whether they say "yes" or "no" becomes more or less irrelevant. But, let me tell you, if you're detached and having a blast, you'll be much more likely to get "yeses."

David and I practice this all of the time. Perhaps it's because we're dating professionals, but when we go out, especially with clients, we simply have a good time. We try out new material, test our latest research, and even seek out the angry or closed-looking women just for a challenge. We have a great time because we've turned the process into something highly enjoyable. Plus, being married, we're not tied to an outcome either.

You aren't doing this for a business or research, but you can start to make it much more fun. In fact, you can get your first taste of it right now! I want you to go out in a public place and approach five women. You can just say, "Hi, how are you?" if you want. Do it with a friend and make it a game. Maybe right now your goal can be just to get them to laugh. Write down your observations.

Hopefully, you won't be like Boomhauer and need twenty-three approaches to get one phone number. However, even if you do, and you try that every weekend throughout the foreseeable future, I can tell you this: your cell phone contacts will be pretty full. And, I bet you'll also never be dateless and lonely again.

Chapter Thirty-One

Building Rapport

We mentioned earlier in the book about how women look for a provider and protector when seeking men. However, this doesn't mean they're looking for some shirtless guy wildly swinging his fists in the street. Because they've been traditionally more vulnerable than men, they're also wired to be much more cautious than we are about whom they'll date.

In terms of their brain evolution, this means you absolutely have to not only impress them with your value, but also make them feel comfortable that you're not going to harm them (or the offspring they might have with you). How can you impress on a girl that you're safe and secure? By building rapport.

Rapport building is also a way to tell her you are even more attractive than your initial impression indicated. Rapport is also important if you want her to feel comfortable with you sexually. Many guys will tell a random girl she is "hot," and come across creepy, while she likes it when other guys call her that. Why? The answer is that a random guy hasn't built any rapport with her first.

So, the rapport building process is important. If you can't master establishing rapport, you're never going to get her in a relationship.

It may be helpful to think of rapport building as getting on the same wavelength with someone else. Have you ever heard someone say, "I like his vibe?" A vibe is a vibration or wave. If you hear a vibration, it's possible to mimic it with your voice or another instrument. By doing this, you would be "on the same wavelength." The girls you want to approach are unique individuals you want to get to know better. Find out their "vibe" and get in tune with it.

Obviously, rapport building is a two-way street. As a man, you will have to take the lead and probably even do most of the work. Remember, it's what women expect; they're the passive participants in most relationships. This is especially true if the girl you've approached is shy. But, you can build rapport with anyone using our tips. The first three come from psychologist and founder of Neurolinguistic Programming (NLP) Richard Bandler.

The first technique is called behavioral mirroring. As the name implies, you will mirror the girl's behavior. You can adjust the pitch of your voice, your position, tone, breathing, speed of talking, posture, movement, etc. to match hers. If she puts her arms on the table, you would do the same. Make sure you're subtle; otherwise it may look weird or appear as if you are mocking her. Mirroring breathing seems to be particularly effective, but also subtle enough that the conscious mind does not notice it.

Sometimes women will mirror your movements, which is actually a sign she might like you. But, if you notice her body language is closed or she appears nervous, modeling open, relaxed behavior for her to mirror will make her more comfortable.

Another good tip is to use symbolic mirroring. This is taking someone else's symbols and using them. An example would be if you want to convince a liberal audience of a conservative point, speak to them using the language of a liberal.

Listen carefully for cues when you first meet people. They often give away their symbolic preferences in conversation. For example, a girl may tell you when discussing her job situation, "I finally see the light at the end of the tunnel." Later in the conversation, when it's your turn, you could use light/tunnel language for explaining your own success. Be creative on this one, but again don't appear to be satirizing or mocking the girls you're trying to win over.

Third, you should try pacing and matching. This is different from mirroring and involves integrating parts of a person's personality, speech, and mannerisms into your own way of communicating. This could involve using another person's vocabulary (you know, like, talking like a teen to reach a teenager), or their "representational system" (e.g. if they are primarily auditory, use phrases such as "I hear you;" if they are primarily visual, say, "I see that," etc.).

You need to listen to how they speak to determine their primary representational system. A "representational system" is how a person processes and expresses his or her thoughts. The choices are visual ("that *looks* great"), auditory ("that *sounds* awesome") and kinesthetic ("that must *feel* rough"). You may even start to do this naturally as the conversation continues. It's amazing how much mirroring occurs naturally in human interaction.

Fourth, another easy way to build rapport is to simply listen. Obviously, there are many cases where you want to talk a lot, like when you approach people in a busy club and want to show them your high-value. However, to build rapport, you'll have to stop and actually listen at some point. You should always have a good mix of showing your personal charm and taking time to hear out the other person.

Extroverted people need to remember this especially since they can come across as domineering, particularly when dealing with shyer individuals. Brief periods of silence are acceptable, especially if one person is more shy.

Fifth, you can build rapport with others by being knowledgeable and well-read. By being able to speak intelligently about a variety of topics, you can instantly connect with many and diverse people. For example, I don't read comic books, but I know about them from my childhood. Once I met a girl who loved comics and that childhood knowledge really helped me get to know her better.

So, make sure you're a well-rounded individual. Be able to talk about topics from science to sports and everything in between, even if it's just enough to fake it. If you have no clue about anything outside of your own personal niches, then good luck meeting anyone outside of your own little world (no short person pun intended).

Sixth, one of the best ways to build rapport is to find commonalities you have with the other person. We tend to bond with those we are similar to. If you see a girl wearing an Imagine Dragons shirt, and you like that band as I do, not only could you approach her based on it ("Hey, do you like the Imagine Dragons?"), but it could be a chance to build some great rapport as you discuss your favorite songs.

During the course of any conversation, finding and emphasizing commonalities help build great rapport. Discover her degree, job, hometown, favorite foods, hangouts, favorite bands, etc., and go from there.

Finally, you should assume rapport. In other words, act like you've already built rapport with the girl you've approached. This belief will affect your own body language and attitude, taking some stress from the situation. After all, you wouldn't have any trouble talking to your friends. Assuming rapport may even "trick" the woman you've met into thinking you already know her or at least have met her at one point in time. Have you ever accidentally given a big "hi, how are ya?" wave to a stranger? Likely they waved in the same way, almost like they knew you, because they were mirroring you. They may still think to this day they knew you from somewhere!

When talking to a woman, realize that they typically focus on emotions, in other words, how they feel about a specific topic. Let's look at an example from sports. My wife went to a high school football game with me once. She enjoyed being in the crowd of people, talking to people she knew, and discussing the patterns on the cheerleading outfits. She also liked how the game was fast-paced and interesting.

However, she didn't care at all about the rules of the game or my attempt to explain them. For her, it was about the emotional experience. Instead of relying on facts and objective observations, men should try to speak to women using what John Alexander, author of How to Become an Alpha Male, calls emotionally relevant language. This means framing your conversations in terms of experiences and your feelings about them.

Let me give you an example. You drive to meet a girl for coffee. Rather than talking about the details of the trip, the specific business deals you made that day, and other facts, explain how you experienced your day and the trip over. You might say, "I saw the coolest thing on the way over," or "I felt really intrigued by something a client said this morning." You've explained your day, but in a way that focuses on experience and emotions.

However, you'll want to avoid being too *emotional*. Emotionalism comes across to a woman as needy, girly, and low-value. An example of emotionalism from the above story would be saying, "I'm so angry at my boss' secretary that I could just punch something." Although it is emotional and is speaking from experience, it just isn't the behavior of a high-value man.

All of these tips are designed to help you do something that David and I try to do with all people we meet: make them feel like they are the complete center of our attention for the brief period that we interact with them. It is not just about making them feel that way either: when we interact with others, they *do* get all of our attention, and the rapport we build shows it to them. If you can have this level of personal charisma, you will have friends and dates flocking to you.

Your assignment for this chapter is to go out and actually build rapport. I know it sounds silly, but try it with someone you know at first. It's low pressure, so you can try the techniques without looking silly or condescending, and you'll probably get to know the person a lot better. You'd be amazed how little rapport often exists between friends and acquaintances. After you test your mettle with some family members or friends, I want you to try it with total (female) strangers. Build rapport with at least two women.

Chapter Thirty-Two

The Close

In spring of 1994, my sophomore year in high school, I spent most of my time hanging with a girl named Angela. Every guy in school liked her, and I was fortunate enough to spend time with her almost every day after school.

I languished in the "friend-zone" with her for about five months. I found out two years later that she liked me. But, at the time, even though we walked the two mile loop to and from a secluded spring outside of town nearly every day (alone!), I just couldn't close and get into a romantic relationship with her. It was crazy. I knew she liked me, but I just couldn't take it to the next level.

You may be master of the approach and rapport building, but if you can't make the close, then you're pretty much out of luck (like me). Failing to make the close will, in social situations, leave you lonely in the long term. Many men, especially short guys, have missed out on relationships with beautiful women because they were too scared to get their contact information or escalate to a romantic level.

There are a variety of psychological reasons why it's hard to make the close, including low self-esteem and anxiety. However, I think for many men, it comes down to a simple lack of confidence: they fear being rejected. It feels pretty bad when you've gotten to know someone and you ask for her number, only to be shot down after all that effort.

Whether you fear the close or not, if you don't make it, you'll miss out on many opportunities since "closing" is absolutely necessary for any success with women, whether it's sex or a long-term relationship. Entertaining girls in one-off approaches can be fun, but you still need those make deeper, lasting connections too. Here are my guidelines for successfully making the close.

First, you must remember that when making the close, it is absolutely your job to do it. If you wait for the girl to give you her number, then you'll be waiting a long time. Some girls will insist on giving you their numbers, but that's the rare example and only if you're a total stud. In the vast majority of cases, you'll have to ask.

Second, you have to get some type of reliable contact information. You don't truly close unless you have her number (ideal) or another way to contact her. I guess this might not apply to one night stands, but those are very rare and I don't recommend them anyway. It's not a close if you don't have a way to contact her later.

You don't have to just come out and say, "Give me your number." In fact, you should probably be a little slicker about it (although the direct approach is sometimes best). Adding a bit of humor and making yourself look good may be helpful too. This could be as easy as saying, "Since I know you had such a good time talking to me, you should give me your number." If you can tell she was enjoying your company, say this confidently and she will love it.

Another easy way to close is through social media. When you're done with the conversation, you can suggest you both be friends on Facebook or other platforms. People are often more comfortable adding friends or followers on social media than giving out their number because these sites offer more options for privacy. In addition, with smart phones, it's possible to add and/or confirm the person right there so you leave the location certain of having made the close.

Third, give the girl a reason to have you contact her. For example, if I meet someone I like and want to get to know better (male and female), I'll typically bring up my business. I'm always looking for graphic designers, extras in photos, etc. and I will sometimes mention this (casually and indirectly, so people aren't scared off).

Sometimes those I'm talking to will express interest in fulfilling my business needs (and making a few bucks in the process), so they want to connect with me and even suggest it. This is because if people think there is a benefit for them, they will happily give you their number, Twitter information, or anything else really. Of course, ideally, the benefit is simply knowing and dating you!

Fourth, practice makes perfect. If you're too scared to practice with girls, then go to a networking event first. You can simply give others your business card. This will get you used to getting numbers (and even approaching and rapport building).

Networking events are ideal for practicing the close because there is an expectation of closing (and approaching too). Men and women attend those events because they expect to give and receive contact information. Since a lot of these events are at bars and social venues, you might even meet a girl there while you're "practicing!"

Fifth, it's best to keep the close process simple. You should get the number or other contact information before the interaction is over. Going back to ask for it later, having someone else get it for you, looking the person up on Facebook when you get home, or any indirect, late, or Rube Goldberg methods (look him up) should be avoided. They make you look timid and lacking in confidence. No girl wants a guy who has to do that kind of ridiculous stunt just to get her number.

Finally, make closing fun. Remain detached, just like you should be doing with the approach and rapport building. Don't act like getting this girl's contact information is going to make or break your life. If she says "no," life goes on. If she says "yes," life goes on. Have fun with the process and be creative. But, above all, closing shouldn't be an anxiety-filled burden.

Also, if you fail to make the close, don't feel bad. It's not always a reflection on the job you did or your value. Maybe she has a jealous boyfriend. Some girls are also just naturally private or loners. She might not even find you attractive. But, that's okay. Move onto another girl. Remember, this is fun and you're going to be getting numbers more often, now that you are becoming confident and attractive.

Your practice assignment is to go out to a club or other popular, social-themed venue or event on a Friday or Saturday night and practice all three aspects of meeting someone new: approaching, building rapport, and closing. Try not to leave without getting her number or at least becoming friends with her on social media. But, the number is better.

Chapter Thirty-Three

Follow-Up

Jim was a great client of ours. One summer Saturday, we took him to a club and winged him. He ended up with a phone number. Since our work was done for the night (so we assumed), we went home. The next day when we called him, he was very upset. The girl wasn't interested! When I asked him when he found out, he told me it was a couple hours after he left the club! He had literally started texting her as soon as he exited the door of the bar.

It's not just the approach, rapport building, and close that must be mastered if you want to date beautiful women. There's also the little (or big) thing called "the follow-up." And, lots of guys (like Jim) struggle with this, especially if they've just met a girl they really like at a club. If that's you, then you're in luck because we can help.

Before I give any advice, you have to remember one thing about the follow-up. Just because you've "closed" you do not already have this woman in your back pocket. In other words, a number doesn't mean you're suddenly her boyfriend or even on that path. There is obviously some attraction or interest. You've succeeded there. Pat yourself on the back! But, having contact information doesn't mean you are guaranteed anything (so keep it to one pat).

The first thing I like to mention about the follow-up is timing. That's the question I most often get asked: when should I follow-up? The answer, as frustrating as it might be, is "it depends." But there are a few things to keep in mind. Above all, you don't want to come across as desperate or over-eager. If you text her right out of the bar (or in the bar) you could appear that way.

Remember that you need to appear high-value and confident. A high-value, confident guy has options. He doesn't desperately jump at any phone number he gets. He's busy. He has things to do and people to see. He's way too occupied with important stuff to quickly text a girl back. Sure, you may want to jump after that one number because you are desperate and have no life, but you must resist that urge.

Generally, you'll hear about the "24 hour rule." In other words, don't text her back for twenty-four hours. That's not bad advice, but it's not necessarily the best. I find that texting her the next day, just so it's not as soon as you wake-up, is generally fine. Wait until the mid-afternoon to show her that it's not your first priority.

While you can wait longer, there's really no need to. You're not appearing desperate, but you're also not coming across as someone trying to wait a particular amount of time. You want to appear naturally confident, not some guy following a rule. Ideally, if you have options, you'll just respond when you feel like the time is right.

Second, you'll want to follow-up in a restrained manner. By this, I mean keep the conversation light and non-committal at the start. If you met her at a club and she had been drinking or living in the moment, she might be waking up to reality. And, she might not like what she remembers of the previous night (even if she liked you then).

If you come out expressing how great of a time you had, the passion you had when kissing, how beautiful she was, etc. you're going to absolutely scare her off. You want to look at the follow-up as reestablishing rapport. You have to rebuild your level of trust with her. You don't have to start from scratch, but proceed slowly.

I recommend a follow-up with something like, "Hey, this is Jonathan from last night. I hope you made it home safely. How's it going?" Notice how, I'm reintroducing myself, asking about her welfare, and also opening up a new conversation. Even if she completely regrets the previous night, she can still respond to this without fear.

Third, you'll want to attempt to get a conversation going with her. Once she responds to your initial question, try to ask some more open ended questions. I advise starting out with casual type of conversation.

Don't ask her back out on the third or fourth text. You need to build up more comfort first.

Fourth, you'll still want to escalate and keep the sexual tension going. You don't want to go into the friend-zone when you know she's attracted to you. Remember, drunken words (or actions) are usually sober thoughts. After you've built some genuine rapport first (very important), throw in a few escalators. Say, "You really looked hot last night," or "You're a really good kisser."

Make sure these comments are contextually appropriate and also don't throw them out until you're absolutely certain she's comfortable talking to you again. You have to time it right: avoid the friend-zone but also avoid being rejected for creepiness.

Fifth, get her back out at some point. If you sense that she still likes you, then it's important that you get the two of you out on a date. Once again, it's best if you start small. Don't invite her out to a romantic dinner. Say something like, "We should have a cup of coffee next week," or something similar. From there, you can show her your value, continue to increase the sexual tension, then maybe move on to something more typically "date" oriented.

Finally, be aware that sometimes you're just not going to get anywhere when you follow-up. Yeah, that's a sad reality of meeting women (especially when they've been drinking). It might have nothing to do with you. Maybe she was just out for one night of fun. She might have a boyfriend (or even a husband!) or be too busy for a relationship in her own mind.

If she's not interested anymore, the signs will likely be there. If she won't respond at all, then she's not interested for sure! But, she also might be courteous and not have the guts to just cut it off. If so, keep an eye out for these: non-committal, short, or abrupt texts. If you know she's not busy, and she still takes a long time responding between texts, then she's likely on the fence or uninterested. She likely has another guy in her life too. Also, if she is always "busy," and can't find even a few hours to meet with you, she isn't that interested.

None of these is indicative that she doesn't like you in some way (except maybe not texting back). So, you can be patient. But, don't pester a girl (which will put her off the fence, on the "not liking you" side). And, if you don't see any interest in a few days, then just give up. Don't tell her that. Just stop texting. If she misses you and really did like you, she'll contact you.

If she doesn't seem interested in pursuing anything further, don't freak out or take it personally. A lot can happen, especially if you met her in a setting that involved alcohol.

People can be strange. Maybe she is dating a loser and meeting you was the best thing that happened to her in ages. But, the next morning she woke up beside the loser and her strong commitment to him rushed back in her head. The familiarity of the loser ultimately beat out the good, but new, feelings you engendered inside of her. Sad? Yes. Does it happen a lot? Yes.

Feel pride that you got a phone number (it means she was attracted to you). Then, armed with that extra confidence, go out the next weekend and get two or three numbers. That way when you follow-up, your odds of success will be much better.

By the way, if you got a social media contact (like Facebook or Twitter), then it's probably best to move on to texting if possible. In today's world most people check texts even more than social media. And, they don't have to be connected to the internet or have a data plan to respond to you.

There's no assignment for this chapter because you might not have gotten a phone number by this point. However, once you get one, make sure to follow the guidelines in this chapter. If you have a phone number, then test out these techniques and see how they work for you.

Chapter Thirty-Four

Dating Tall Girls

My sophomore year in college, I met Michelle, a resident assistant at my dorm. She was a pretty girl with a nice personality. She was also interested in me. I'm not sure why since I wouldn't nail down the skills I'm teaching you until a few years later. But, we managed to have a fairly brief relationship.

What's interesting about Michelle (other than the fact that she dated me when I was at my most pathetic!) was her height. I think she had about five inches on me. And, she had absolutely no problem with it. The only person who felt insecure was me!

If you're short, especially if you're really short, you will probably be dating a taller woman at some point in your life. A quick glance at "short support" type forums shows that many short guys are scared to death of dating taller women. I'm not sure why, since I believe that taller women are actually more open to dating short men. I'll explain why and then give a few tips for landing and dating a taller girl.

I believe taller girls are more open to dating shorter men for a couple of reasons. First, taller girls are more likely to have more testosterone than shorter females. These high testosterone women act and think more like men. It doesn't mean they're ugly or masculine, just that their thought patterns and choices are more in line with traditionally masculine thinking.

And, how do men typically act towards women? They take a "the more, the better" attitude. Men are generally less picky about women then women are about guys. Men are much more likely to be promiscuous (maybe we should say, "More open to relationships of a physical nature"). Likewise, high testosterone women are less choosy and thus more likely to break away from the standard norms of society. Thus, they'll likely give short guys much more of a chance than the high estrogen girl who insists on a tall, dark, and handsome provider.

Second, taller girls often suffer from some of the same insecurities as shorter men. They have experienced similar problems with bullying, not being able to find clothes that fit, etc. As a result, many taller women are less likely to hold to as rigid standards as the more "mainstream" women who always had social benefits handed to them because of their traditionally feminine beauty. Tall girls also don't get as much attention from guys, and may be more open to your advances.

This doesn't mean that taller women are guaranteed to date you. Everyone is unique. And, some women don't like to "tower over" their boyfriends, so that may be an issue. Also, a tall girl's insecurities could get the best of her. You never know. My main point is that you should never discount taller women and assume they would never date you.

The point of this book is this: if you want to date her, no matter her height, good looks, etc. then you have the skills to do it. Will you face rejection at times? Of course! But, you'll also face success a lot too!

Also, taller women can sometimes, like men, be more aggressive and actually pursue you, rather than the other way around. While that can be fun, it should never be a crutch for not learning the skills of approach, rapport, and close. For example, Michelle pretty much approached and closed with me. But, when she was gone, I was back to square one. And, it sucked.

There are a few things you should keep in mind when trying to date tall women. This advice will make your life much easier and you'll find more overall success with them.

First, realize that just as you might feel the need to cover your own insecurities, tall girls might feel the need to do the same thing. Be patient. For instance, you might not want her to wear heels because it makes you look short, but she might need them to feel feminine. You should always be the secure one in the relationship no matter her insecurities. This applies to every relationship you have.

Second, you might get some crap from others about the height difference. Or she might get it, even from her supposed friends. Once again, be secure with yourself. Don't let the haters get to you as long as you're both happy. In many cases, it's probably jealousy, especially if you truly are a happy couple. Some people really can be petty.

Finally, the height difference might make certain, ahem, aspects of the relationship a little difficult. For example kissing and sexual activity could require some adjustments. Just do your best on that and be creative. Happiness and sexual compatibility aren't contingent on being at eye level.

Your assignment is to go out and talk to one tall girl. Approach her and try out some of what you've learned in this book (humor, etc.). I want you to see how tall girls are just like any other girl and maybe even easier to win over. Some tall girls get so blown away by the confidence of short guy approaching them that the act alone makes them fall in love with you! Write down your observations.

Chapter Thirty-Five

What About Online Dating?

Eric, one of our first clients, didn't have many skills when we met him after he attended one of our dating talks. In spite of his admission of weakness, he still expressed how he didn't need our services because he was going to find the love of his life online. I wished him the best, but reminded him that online dating had its own pitfalls. He disagreed.

Two months later he emailed me and told me that not only hadn't he found the love of his life, but he'd spent nearly two hundred dollars trying his hand at online dating. Sadly, he didn't just not find his true love; he also had a grand total of zero dates to show for his money and effort. And, only one girl even responded to his messages and that was to tell him that she wasn't interested in him romantically. Fortunately, he had the courage to ask us for help. Most guys don't.

Online dating seems like it would be great for guys whose dating skills in the real world are lackluster. And, it does have a few advantages. For one, it allows time. An awkward guy in real life has the ability to craft a great profile and can respond to messages with forethought and wit. He might not be as quick on the draw in real life. And, he can meet a lot of different girls since online dating isn't geographically limiting.

A guy with skills and the right measurements and looks can have a lot of success with internet dating. However, an average looking guy with no skills? For him, believe it or not, online dating can actually be worse than the real world. Here's why.

First, dating online requires the same skill set as real world dating. You think hot women online will accept a low-value nice guy who can't impress them? Not at all. So, that means on the internet you still have to be valuable, witty, edgy, and so forth. While some guys can develop an online persona that they don't have in real life, most just fall totally flat in both places.

Second, while the internet dating world appears to be much larger and diverse than "real world" options, there's also much more competition. So, when you search a dating site, there are five hundred girls online in your metro area. Great! But there are probably two thousand guys. That's right, with online dating, guys typically outnumber girls anywhere from five to thirty to one! The dating websites won't tell you that, but it's true. What does that mean?

It means that girls online are very choosy, especially the pretty ones. Basic economics says that they will use their choice to sort out lower-value guys. Ladies we work with in our business tell us that when they went online to get dates, they would literally wake up to hundreds of messages in their mailbox. Yes, *hundreds*. They couldn't even read them all! So, in the case of Eric, of the messages he sent to girls (to the tune of two hundred dollars), only twenty to thirty might even have been opened.

Finally, online dating is great for women, but bad for men. Not only do women get inundated with attention by a bunch of guys, but they can also choose the "pick of the litter!" But, it gets worse for guys. In real life, women typically judge men on more intangible elements like charm, confidence, and body language. What is it difficult to show online? Did you say charm, confidence, and body language? If so, give yourself an "A."

Thus, what aspect do women typically focus on when they're dating on the internet? Looks. That's right. They start to care more about looks, which can be clearly shown online, at least to determine if you get a first date. And, the standards they have are ridiculous. They want a guy who is tall, dark, handsome, has a killer body, etc. And…when they're receiving a hundred messages a day, they can weed out anyone who doesn't meet all 125 crazy requirements. Average guys lose.

This is why online dating is especially perilous for short men. These sites encourage women to "check boxes." And, the one box they almost always check is "tall." Some sites offer women a minimum height requirement. And, there are dating websites that even allow them to filter by height. So, she might not even receive your messages or show up in your search results if you're not over six foot.

My advice for men, especially short men, is this regarding online dating: you can do it, but only as a part of a broader dating strategy. So, if you're reading this book, improving your skills, and raising your value, then you have a chance to succeed online. But, remember, it's tougher. You have to try it in that mindset, as a fun challenge.

So, if you decide to try your hand at online dating, then good for you. But, keep a few things in mind. Here are the tips we give to our clients.

First, when you create an online profile, put yourself in the best light and appear high-value. So, make yourself look confident, successful, witty, and worth dating. You have time, so use it. Don't come across as a braggart, but let the girls know that you have things going for you.

Don't say too much, though, because you don't want women to find a red flag and disqualify you in favor of the other fifty guys messaging them. In person, intangible elements might keep her attracted even if you say something dumb. You say it online? You're just going to turn her off. Say just enough in your profile to let them know you're valuable. A little mystery always helps a guy look attractive anyway.

Second, always put the best spin on your situation, but never resort to an outright lie. If you're short, don't imply you're tall. If you work at McDonald's, don't hint that you're a high-powered businessman. In person lying is a lot tougher, but when doing online dating, it's all too easy.

If your goal is anything beyond getting emails from dating sites, then you will be facing the girl in real life. And, those lies? Well, they'll likely come back to bite, especially if they're whoppers and you don't live up to her expectations. Not only that, but lying about yourself shows you're insecure. And, no girl wants to date an insecure man.

Third, be funny and creative with your profile (but in a high-value way) and your messages. When you contact women, make sure you show your confidence and uniqueness. Remember, she's getting tons of messages. Yours must be different in a positive way.

Fourth, choose a good, flattering photo that is straightforward and recent. Weird angles, outdated photos, and other tricks only tell women that you're attempting to trick them. Show your best, but real self and let the chips fall. It'll make you look confident and secure in your looks.

One good way to stick out is to be witty (even teasing her) based on her profile. It makes you look confident and funny and it shows you paid attention to her. Lots of guys just send the same random message to every girl, and it usually goes something like, "Oh you are so beautiful I just had to message you and tell you this ;)."

It makes them look careless, needy, overly "nice," and boring. While this advice to tease her may not be enough to win her over, it'll at least get you a second look. When she's bombarded with hundreds of messages, this is a huge advantage. Oh, and never use a smiley face, except perhaps a wink. Women use them, not guys.

Finally, all online dating should be done with the real world in mind. So, whatever you do, always be moving the relationship towards real life encounters. If you get into a good conversation on Facebook, try to get her out for coffee. If you get some fun text messaging going, invite her out after a couple of days.

In fact, you should get her out sooner than later. Don't come across as demanding or needy, but, aware of your competition, you should always move to an encounter in person sooner than later. If you wait around and delay, there's going to be another guy who won't wait. And, he's going to get the girl while you dither.

I want to say an extra word about height since this is a short man's dating guide. How should you handle the height issue? Lie. Okay, I know I said not to do that earlier. But, I want to you to lie slightly about your height. Here's why this is an exception to the rule: a little bit of lying is absolutely expected when doing online dating. Women almost always lie about their weight (and even age) on dating websites. You can play that game too.

Add one to two inches to your height, especially if you're really short. Don't go any taller, though. And, when you first meet her, wear shoes with a decent heel or boots. That way, you're not going to appear too much smaller.

Why should you do this? Because she'll give you a greater chance of a first date (or even a return message) if you add those inches. Then, when you get out with her, you can wow her with your high-value personality and other physical characteristics. If you do this right, she won't care about the extra two inches you added. She might not even notice. You can return the favor and ignore the fact that she's put on three pounds and aged a year since her picture.

These tips should help you get started with online dating. But, remember the pitfalls as well. However, if you're up for a challenge, go for it. Eric, after our coaching, received dates both in the real world and online.

Your assignment for this chapter is to update your online profile (if you have one) in accord with what you learned in this chapter (and book). If you don't date online, then keep this information in the back of your head in case you decide to pursue it in the future.

Chapter Thirty-Six

Conclusion

Hey shorty! How's the view from down there? Okay, that's a joke because unless you're below 5′6″, you won't be looking up to me (literally) anytime soon. Does me saying that still bother you? I hope that you can brush it off, or at least act like it doesn't bug you. If you can't get over it, then maybe you need to re-read a few chapters.

Hopefully the material in this book is changing your life. But, unless you're the perfect student, it likely hasn't totally changed your life yet. But, even by now, you should be noticing some significant changes. At the very least you should be more confident and high-value. And, you should be projecting this to people (especially women) you meet and already know.

But, remember that you're involved in the process of change. It takes some time and effort. You've been short with low self-esteem for a long time. You're not going to totally transform yourself into the world's greatest romantic player overnight. But, over several months, you should see a huge difference. At the very least life should start to be a hell of a lot more fun.

David and I wrote this book for two reasons. First, we actually enjoy writing and teaching dating material. It is our specialty and business. But, the primary reason is that we believe in helping guys. We were both men who had absolutely no confidence in dating women. And, it led to constant misery and frustration.

Now, however, we are incredibly good at meeting women (and men) and teaching guys how to do it too. In fact, our transition from loser to awesome has been nothing short of amazing. We feel the excitement of success instead of the pain of defeat (or the frustration of not even playing).

There isn't a day that goes by that we don't reflect in gratitude about how much our lives have changed for the better. We love it when other guys feel the same way we do now. And, it's even more awesome when they go out and meet the girls of their dreams.

We urge you to visit our main website, thepopularman.com, and take advantage of hundreds of free articles and other resources. We also would love it if you visited confidencedelivery.com and signed up for our newsletter, to get regular tips like the ones in this book. New research related to dating, social psychology, etc., emerges daily, and we keep track of everything so you don't have to! Our newest site, verticalimpact.net has articles and stories specifically related to dating and life success for shorter guys. I believe you'll find all of these sites helpful in your continued process of transformation.

So, we wish you the best in dating! Your height, or your insecurity about your height, doesn't have to control your destiny any more. Of course, if you follow the principles in this book, you won't need luck. You will have skills to get any girl you want.

APPENDIX A

ELEVEN TOP TEASES

This list first appeared in similar form in another book of ours, Eleven Dating Mistakes Guys Make (And How To Correct Them). We highly recommend you get that book for general dating ideas related to the concepts in this book.

Teasing girls in a playful and flirtatious way is very important to winning them over romantically. Avoid using these in serious environments (like work, networking events, etc.) where flirting is not expected and may get in the way of professional interaction.

Below I have listed eleven "teases" or "negs" that signal you are being flirtatiously confident, which is very important when interacting with women you are attracted to. I also have included a brief tip about following up these teases.

The examples below are just to get you started. You have to carry on the flirting from there! And remember, these must be delivered playfully and confidently. A general rule of thumb is don't insult her intelligence. Teasing about that rarely works. Avoid teasing about death, killing, cruelty, prejudice, and sexually suggestive things. She needs to feel safe and secure. Don't be a creep or a jerk! Also, you may have to "soften" these for women who are older or that aren't as used to being flirted with (e.g. less pretty women). Use common sense.

1. You Know What I Like About You?

Situation:

A girl has said something that is offensive, even if it is only slightly offensive and/or unintended, including something about your height.

Example:

You approach a girl and start talking to her about your job. You volunteer you are an engineer, and to be snarky she says, "Oh, you are an engineer…so you operate trains?" You reply, "You know what I like about you?" You pause for a moment as if to think, and answer, "nothing really." Alternatively, you can draw it out by saying, "You know what I like about you?" and pause and say, "Wait, give me a minute…I can do this!"

Comments:

This works in part because when you get ready to say what you like about her, 99% of the time, people follow with a compliment. She is expecting a compliment. You are interrupting her normal train of thought, and being funny and charming as well. This one wins on a variety of levels. Just keep it flirtatious!

2. Judge Judy (Thanks to Joshua Wagner for this one)

Situation:

When a girl says something judgmental to you, even if slightly.

Example:

You are ordering at a coffee shop. You order Hazelnut flavoring. The barista says, "Ugh that is gross." You reply, "Hey, put down your gavel, Judge Judy!" Alternatively, you could respond, "Hey, did I ask your opinion, Judy?" She will reply, "Judy, that's not my name!" You reply, "Oh, well from the way you were judging me, I thought your name had to be 'Judge Judy.'"

Comments:

Make sure she knows you are flirting and not actually accusing her of being judgmental.

3. Name Change (Thanks to Joshua Wagner for this one)

Situation:

This works in any situation where you have been interacting with a girl for a while, and you know her name (such as a waitress or girl you have met).

Example:

Your waitress named Maria asks you how your food tastes. You say, "Oh it tastes great, Miranda." Nearly all the time, she will reply, "Miranda! My name is Maria!" A good follow-up to her comment is something like this: "Oh…well I like Miranda better, you should go with that instead."

Comments:

You have to be confident with this one. She has to know you're flirting and not actually forgetful or dumb. Also, by suggesting she go by a new name you are showing lots of confidence.

4. I Don't Recall Asking For Any Sass (Thanks to Joshua Wagner for this one)

Situation:

Any time a girl questions something you do, even slightly, especially when she works in a service job.

Example:

You order a hamburger and fries at McDonalds or another restaurant before lunch is officially served. The employee responds, "Oh we can't serve you until 10:30." You reply, "I asked for a side of fries, not a side of sass…geez."

Comments:

The word "sass" just sounds funny. Make sure to use this one while you are in a happy and confident mood. You have to clearly convey you aren't really mad. This one works best when the girl hasn't actually said something really offensive. This indicates that you are flirting. Also, most women consider being called "sassy" a compliment.

5. Without The Attitude?

Situation:

A girl is doing something for you (delivering food, turning in something, etc.) and has a pretend bad attitude about it, i.e. she is flirting.

Example:

A waitress is flirting with you. When you ask for ketchup she says, "Man, you are demanding!" You reply, "You know what really tastes good? Ketchup delivered without attitude." Alternatively, maybe she gave you a hard time about needing a drink refill. When she delivers your drink, have a quick sip and say, "Mmm, I can really tell you delivered this with a bad attitude. I can taste it…very bitter."

Comments:

There are a variety of ways to word this one. Just make sure the whole mood is flirtatious. Don't exasperate a waitress or your food might have things in it you don't want! This one works best if she is pretending to give you an attitude for flirting purposes.

6. "You Don't Like Me; You Love Me"

Situation:

A girl seems to be into you, but has just said she doesn't like you.

Example:

You are talking with a woman, and it seems to be going well. However, she says, "You know, I don't know if I like you." You respond, "You're right; you don't like me. You love me."

Comments:

This works because you seem to agree with her ("You're right; you don't like me…"), but then take it in a direction she isn't expecting. It shows humor and confidence, and is a great way to flirt with a girl who has just expressed her possible dislike of you. If a girl really, truly doesn't like you, this one might backfire. I suggest using this one when most signs point to her liking you, even if she throws out the "I don't like you" comment.

7. Grading Her

Situation:

When a woman is doing something that can be evaluated, like making coffee, serving food, telling you something, etc.

Example:

You order a cup of coffee, and the female barista tells you about the different types of coffee and new store promotions. After paying, just before you walk away, you thank her and say, "You know, you are a great barista. I give you a B-." She will almost always reply with fake indignation, saying, "Only a B-??" You reply, "Oh okay, maybe you're right…you earned a solid 'B.'"

Comments:

The key to making this work is to take someone who has done a great job and give her a lower "grade" than expected. Usually a C+, B-, and B+ are good "grades." Don't go too low or the joke goes from fun to offensive. Be ready to raise or lower the grade based on her response to your initial grade. If she gives you a little playful attitude, lower her grade, and explain that her attitude caused that. If she says something like "Hey now!" raise it slightly, but still keep it lower than she wants. Keep it fun; she has to know you are playing and not judging.

8. Whoa, I Didn't Ask For Your Life Story

Situation:

When a girl is explaining something to you, and gets a little wordy.

Example:

A girl is explaining to you how she ended up in the teaching field. After she has told you some of the story, interrupt her playfully and say, "Whoa now, I asked for a story, not your life story!" You may want to follow-up by saying, "Okay, enough about you; let's get back to talking about me."

Comments:

Keep this one playful. She has to know you are playing or she will see you as rude. Give her a chance later to finish her story.

9. Can You Repeat That?

Situation:

When a girl is rattling off some type of decently long list, such as beers on tap, flavors of wing sauce, coffee selections, theme options for the school dance, etc.

Example:

A bartender is telling you the list of all the domestic beers they have. She rattles off about eight of them. You look at her as if you have been thinking, and say, "Oh, I'm sorry; I was thinking about something that happened at work today; can you repeat that?" She expresses some indignation. Don't let her actually repeat the list. Immediately say, "I'm just joking; I was really paying attention. I'll take (blank)" and then be sure to name a beer that wasn't on the list.

10. I Really Love Your...It Reminds Me Of...

Situation:

A girl around you is getting complimented a lot for something new, like a hairstyle, clothing item, etc.

Example:

A woman just got a new blondish-brown hair dye. Everyone around her is complimenting her. You chime in and say, "Oh I love your hair! It looks great. My mom's tuna noodle casserole was the exact same color, and man, did I love that dish."

Comments:

The pattern here is to set her up for a compliment and then deliver a tease. It works on a variety of levels. However, be very very very very very careful using something like this. You may really tick her off or come across as creepy. Make sure she knows you are flirting.

11. Why Are You Telling Me What To Do? (Thanks to Joshua Wagner for this one)

Situation:

A woman is telling you what to do, such as a hotel clerk asking you to sign your bill or a hostess telling you to follow her to the table.

Example:

A hostess says, "Have a nice day" as you leave a restaurant. You reply, "Why are you trying to tell me what to do?" You should add something else funny, like "Man, you are pretty bossy!" or "I mean, come on, we just met, and you're already ordering me around. Man!"

Comments:

Like all teases, keep it flirty and confident.

Following Up A Tease

Following up a tease can be tough. Do you reveal you are teasing or do you stay serious? My view is that you want to *kind of* let them know you are just teasing, but still keep the tension there that you might actually be serious.

Let's say you just used the tease when you compared a girl's hair color to your mom's casserole. You might follow with, "Oh, I'm just kidding…I mean, I'm clearly a great guy, right? And a great guy would never say something like that." Say this line with utter confidence, and guess what? She won't really know if you mean it or not, but she will probably give you the benefit of the doubt. This allows for her to have safety and security, but keeps the mystery and tension alive, which are necessary for romantic attraction.

There is no real assignment for the appendix, but obviously you need to go out and practice these teases, as well as come up with your own. Make it so you can deliver these and your original ones with natural ease.

APPENDIX B

RESPONSES TO "SHIT TESTS" AND CRAPPY COMMENTS

I have included lots of responses in this chapter to help you deal with crappy comments from both men and women. This section alone is worth the price of the book; trust me. You may want to memorize some of these outright, so you have quality comebacks handy at all times. You'll also want to think of your own.

Handling Comments From Women

As I mentioned previously, your height will often be the biggest objection a woman throws out when either "testing" you or outright trying to be crappy. So while a tall guy might get criticized on his personality or facial features, when a woman puts you down, it will likely be height-related.

Sometimes, she may be attracted to you, and be "testing" you (see Chapter 25). Unfortunately, other times she may be trying to be mean. Sometimes women will criticize your height in an offhand way, without realizing how much pointing out our short stature bothers us. Either way, the response to these tests is the same: stay charming, confident, and aloof. Don't get mean or bothered: that looks insecure and weak.

Below are common comments she may make about your height, with great responses. It is your responsibility to show her in your body language and general demeanor that she isn't bothering you. These lines can't necessarily help you with that, but the rest of the book can Learn these so you can pull them out any time you need them.

Consider these quotes to belong to general categories that you can apply in a variety of situations. For example, our responses to "Hey midget" can be used any time that word gets thrown at you. We have included more humorous and edgy responses that are noted as such.

This is important, so read carefully. The edgy responses are best used in informal, crowded, and high-pressure settings, like bars or clubs, and may be "too much" for less intense social settings. Avoid them in professional environments. Some of the edgy responses should only be used if you can pull them off in a way that doesn't come across as mean or upset. Remember, sometimes a woman may blurt out comments (such as, "You're shorter than I thought," if this is the first time meeting you in person) and not mean anything bad by them. She may just genuinely be surprised by your height, but still like you. Also, sometimes women may criticize your height as an awkward way of flirting. We suggest using the edgy responses in a flirtatious and funny, but assertive, way, without coming across as angry or bitter.

"Sorry, but I don't date guys who are under six foot."

- "That's a shame. You get to miss out on the privilege of being with me."

- *Edgy*: "That's okay; I have dating preferences that don't include you."

"Hey Midget."

- "Wow, your friends were 100% right…you are uncool."

- *Edgy:* "That sounds kinky. I have always had this 'Wizard of Oz' fantasy where I play a munchkin…Can you play Dorothy?"

"I hate manlets."

- "If you quit being so uncool, this 'manlet' may let you prove what a man he is.'"

- *Edgy:* "For some reason my last girlfriend stopped calling me that after we had sex…something about how I dominated her so well."

"You are cute, but I think I'm too tall for you."

- "That's too bad. You actually had a shot with me until you said that."

- *Edgy:* "Well, I hear women shrink as they age, so look me up when you're eighty…but don't get jealous if I'm dating some hot eighteen year old."

- *Edgy*: Look her up and down and say, "Yeah, now that you mention it, you are too tall for me."

"You're kind of short for me."

- "Yeah, I'm kind of short, but extra awesome. My self-esteem is taller than I am."

- *Edgy:* "My last girlfriend said that too…until we made out, and then for some reason after that it didn't matter anymore."

- *Edgy*: "And your attitude is a little hostile for my tastes, so let's compromise and go on a date and see what happens."

"You're shorter than I expected."

- "You're a little more uncool than I expected, but I'm willing to overlook it."

- "Short? My friends call me 'hightower.' But then again, I usually hang out with midgets."

- *Edgy:* "You're a little sassier than I expected, but I'll lower my standards just this one time."

"You'd be cute if you were a little taller."

- "I can assure you I am cute regardless of my height. At least that is what my girlfriends tell me."

- *Edgy:* "Are you saying you want me to wear high heels? Kinkyyyy…but what the heck…I'm game if you are."

- *Edgy:* "You'd be hot if you were a little less…um…never mind."

"Why can't I find any tall guys to date??"

- "I don't know. Being so tall you'd think they'd be easy to see. Now me, I'm not as easy to find, but once you find me…well…I'll let you find out on your own."

- *Edgy:* "Well, it could be because you're so…well…never mind."

<u>"Tall guys are so hot."</u>

- "Yeah, tall guys are all right, if you manage to find a confident one."

- "Yeah, so hot. It must be because they are so tall, they are closer to the sun."

- "Yeah, I don't have the 'tall' part down, but I have definitely mastered being 'hot.'"

<u>"Hey, calm down Napoleon!"</u>

- "Thanks. I do get all the women I want, but I haven't conquered all of Europe yet."

- *Edgy:* "Thanks, but the only French I have mastered is kissing."

<u>"I want to marry a tall guy so my kids won't be short."</u>

- "If you marry me, they won't necessarily be very tall, but they'll be super-hot."

- "Just marry me and we'll pump our kids full of vitamins and pray for the best."

- *Edgy:* "Oh…you think someone will want to marry you? Interesting. "

Handling Comments From Men

Men sometimes use height as a way to bully or bug each other. Men often tease their buddies. If a guy-friend humorously gives you "crap" about your height, jokingly give him crap back. If he says, "Come on, let's go shorty," you can say, "Sure, I'll be right there, dickwad." This is what guys do. Don't let your insecurity stop you from engaging in typical male banter.

However, when a guy you don't know or like gives you crap, that is different. Cool guys don't tease or put down guys they don't know. So, if a guy is picking on you, that is different from engaging in edgy male banter with your buddies. Getting picked on by a stranger or bully demands a different response.

Also, male-to-male interaction is often more physical, which is why I always suggest having some basic fighting and self-defense skills, just in case standing up to a jerk results in some type of physical altercation. I suggest finding a local martial arts studio that provides focused instruction. As mentioned previously, my brother and I use the online program from The "Self-Defense Company" (myselfdefensetraining.com). It is focused and intense, and should provide the skills to respond if someone physically harasses you.

It is crucial when dealing with male bullies that your body language shows you mean business. When interviewed, criminals and bullies indicate they prey on people who look weak. For many guys, short stature is an automatic sign of your weakness.

Personally I prefer to defuse idiots with humor and words, but sometimes you might have to get physical, although we suggest *never* escalating it that way yourself, but if you need to defend yourself, be ready for it. Below are some things guys might say, and some ways to respond.

I suggest saying them firmly, but with a humorous edge, and showing in your cocky and calm body language that you are ready to back your words up with physical force if the jerk physically escalates. If you respond this way, I find that jerk guys often respect you. Their buddies will roar with laughter, and they'll recognize subconsciously that you just showed yourself to be the boss.

<u>"Hey shorty (midget, etc.)."</u>

- "Shorty? All my girls call me 'Biggie.'"

- "I may be short, but to quote your girlfriend, 'Big things come in small packages.'"

<u>"Pick him last; He's too short."</u>

- "Yeah, pick me last. I'm scheduled to make out with your girlfriend in a few minutes, and I don't want to interrupt that with a basketball game."

- "That's cool. I like defying expectations."

"You're just the perfect size for me to rest my arm on!"

- "I'm not into gay stuff like that, but I'll let your girlfriend know you are."

- "I'm also the perfect size to punch you in the balls, but you might enjoy that too much, so I'll pass."

"Calm down Napoleon!"

- "Thanks, but I haven't conquered all of Europe…yet."

- "Yeah, I can see the comparison…we both have lots of women throwing themselves at us."

- "Napoleon was actually one of Europe's most popular and capable leaders. I'm just like him…well minus the Syphilis."

(In Line) "I don't know if you're tall enough to get on this ride."

- "I don't know if you're smart enough to get on this ride. Fastening your seat belt can be kind of tricky."

- "Oh, I thought this was the line to make out with your girlfriend."

Handling General Discriminatory Comments

There are also general examples of "heightism" you will have to deal with. People often think that it is okay to put down short people, even though they'd never, in our climate of political correctness, treat other groups like this.

Personally, I am not much into claiming "victim" status, but it is nonetheless important to have responses ready whenever general anti-short comments come up. You will want these responses to be less edgy but assertive nonetheless.

Keep in mind that many people aren't trying to be jerks when they make general comments about height. One recent incident is when my co-worker was getting ready to meet with a local police detective. When she saw him from a distance she asked, "So who is the little weasel?" Some co-workers and I immediately corrected her and let her know that he was probably one of the toughest guys we have met. She apologized and even paid extra attention to him.

Remember to stay calm and detached. Yelling or lecturing her would have been very ineffective. Nicely, but firmly, asserting the truth, and defending the value of a guy who had a lot going for him was much more effective.

"You must be mistaken. He can't be the manager; he's too short."

- "He's an accomplished manager actually. Everyone likes him and he gets the job done."

- "I didn't know there was a height requirement to be a great leader."

"I can't believe that actor (athlete, etc.) is so short!"

- "Height has nothing to do with talent. He is accomplished."

- "Yeah he is great at what he does. Height has nothing to do with it."

"I feel sorry for him because he is so short"

- "Why would you feel sorry for him? He's awesome."

- "Yeah…you know with proper medical care short people can live relatively normal lives."

APPENDIX C

A BASIC PRE-DATE CHECKLIST

Some guys reading this may have never gone on a date, or have blown it in the past when they went on one. This is a brief appendix to remind you how to get ready for that first date, and beyond. In order to be your best self, these grooming and dressing tips should apply to you at all times.

As I mention in another book, Eleven Dating Mistakes Guys Make (And How To Correct Them), it is best to *not* think of going out with a girl as a "date."

Calling it a "date" creates all kinds of crazy expectations and pressure. Instead, view it as hanging out with a girl with whom you want romantic engagement. In terms of attitude, you should be your best self (as I've explained throughout this book), as you are at all times. Remember to stay detached. Your life doesn't depend on this, either positively or negatively.

Grooming and Hygiene

- Shower a few hours before you meet her.

- Shave your face right after getting out of the shower (or in it). If you want some stubble, shave the night before.

- Shave your body the day before if you are really hairy and want to get rid of body hair. If you do it a day before, there won't be any hair or any razor marks.

- Use face and hand moisturizer if these are really dry. This is especially true in the winter.

- Wear deodorant and apply cologne (but don't overdo it). If the date is for a long period of time, you can bring along deodorant to reapply it, if needed.

- Make sure your fingernails and toenails are trimmed properly.

- Right before you go out, brush your teeth, floss, and use mouthwash to ensure you have decent breath. I suggest also buying a "tongue scraper" which removes tongue bacteria that cause bad breath. You might want to bring a travel toothbrush and toothpaste and brush after your meal.

- Trim your eyebrows, nose hair, and ear hair if they are out-of-control. Check for boogers.

- Get rid of the "unibrow" if you have one.

- Ensure your hair is styled to some degree, but not overdone.

- Clean out your ears to get rid of any obvious wax build-up.

-Bring mint chewing gum for after dinner or other times when you're with her.

Clothes

- Make sure your clothes fit, match, and generally look sharp.

- Avoid wearing goofy clothes (like T-Shirts with dumb jokes), or clothes that blatantly scream "low-value" (like your Star Wars shirt), unless you know she is really into those things.

- Ensure your clothes are properly washed and aren't too wrinkled. Put any wrinkled clothes in the dryer for ten minutes or until the wrinkles are released. Make sure your clothes smell fresh, and not like mildew, etc.

- Wear a good belt, watch, and nice shoes. Make sure your shoes smell good. I find spraying them with some bleach cleaner and letting them sit for a while helps get rid of unpleasant smells.

- Always wear shoes with a bit of a heel on your first few dates. Give yourself an extra height advantage.

- If it is colder, wear a jacket that makes you look classy.

Other

- Clean your car. Vacuum it, and if hasn't had them in a while, give it a wash and wax.

- Bring enough money to pay for things. Don't try to buy her love. So avoid expensive activities, showing up with a dozen roses, etc., until you know she is attracted to you.

- When deciding where to go for your date, let her know you are confident: *you* make the decision.

- If you are picking her up, show her you are assertive and in control by walking to her door and walking her to your car.

- If you meet her at a restaurant, take charge and make arrangements when you arrive, by giving *your* name for the reservation.

- Don't overeat or drink too much alcohol if you are out on a dinner date.

- Put away your technology. You job is to "wow" her with your presence. If you can't stop checking your phone, you look nervous and disengaged.

- Make the first move romantically. If things are going well, grab her hand, put your arm around her, lean in for a kiss, etc. It is *your* responsibility to make the first move. If she isn't interested, she will tell you or pull away.

Sexy Time

- If you anticipate a sexual encounter or if it's a possibility, make sure your apartment or house is clean and female friendly. In other words, sweep, scrub, and put away your low value crap.

- If you take her somewhere for sexual activity, you will be required to take the lead. Start slowly, then push the envelope in baby steps. You must escalate, just move at a steady pace and only with her approval.

- Only act with her implied consent. In other words, if she shows hesitation or outright blocks you (words or body language), then stop immediately. Move back to what she has allowed and enjoy that. Do not push her beyond what she is comfortable. Any lack of consent is sexual assault or rape.

APPENDIX D

WORKS CITED AND SUGGESTED READING

What follows are the resources that I've referenced throughout this book, and other books that will help you learn more about the various subjects in this book.

Body Language

Driver, Janine, and Mariska Van Aalst. You Say More Than You Think. New York: Crown, 2010.

Navarro, Joe, and Marvin Karlins. What Every Body Is Saying: An Ex-FBI Agent's Guide To Speed-Reading People. New York: Collins Living, 2008.

Pease, Allan, and Barbara Pease. The Definitive Book Of Body Language. New York: Bantam, 2006.

Changing Your Perspective And Brain

Bennett, David, Jonathan Bennett, and Joshua Wagner. Say It Like You Mean It: How To Use Affirmations And Declarations To Create The Life You Want. Columbus, OH: Theta Storm Press, 2011.

Bandler, Richard, and Garner Thomson. The Secrets to Being Happy. IM Press Inc., 2011.

Pert, Candace B. Molecules of Emotion: Why You Feel the Way You Feel. New York: Touchstone, 1999.

Schwartz, Jeffrey, and Sharon Begley. The Mind and the Brain: Neuroplasticity and the Power of Mental Force. New York: HarperCollins, 2003.

Schwartz, Jeffrey, and Rebecca Gladding. You Are Not Your Brain: The 4-step Solution for Changing Bad Habits, Ending Unhealthy Thinking, and Taking Control of Your Life. New York: Avery, 2011.

Communication And Persuasion

Cialdini, Robert. Influence: Science And Practice. Boston: Pearson, 2009.

Garner, Alan. Conversationally Speaking. Los Angeles: Lowell House, 1997.

O'Connor, Joseph, and John Seymour. Introducing NLP: Psychological Skills for Understanding and Influencing People. San Francisco: Conari, 2011.

Rosenberg, Marshall. Nonviolent Communication: A Language Of Life: Create Your Life, Your Relationships, And Your World In Harmony With Your Values. Encinitas, CA: Puddledancer Press, 2008.

Confidence

Alexander, John. How To Become An Alpha Male. Raleigh, NC: Lulu, 2005.

McKenna, Paul, and Michael Neill. I Can Make You Confident: The Power To Go For Anything You Want! New York: Sterling, 2010.

Dating

Bennett, David, and Jonathan Bennett. Eleven Dating Mistakes Guys Make (And How To Correct Them). Lancaster, OH: Theta Hill Press, 2013.

Evolutionary Psychology And Attraction

Badcock, C. R. Evolutionary Psychology: A Critical Introduction. Cambridge, UK: Polity, 2000.

Brizendine, Louann. The Female Brain. New York: Broadway, 2006.

Brizendine, Louann. The Male Brain. New York: Broadway, 2010.

Wright, Robert. The Moral Animal: Evolutionary Psychology and Everyday Life. New York: Vintage, 1995.

Health, Fitness, And Good Looks

King, Ian, and Lou Schuler. The Book of Muscle: The World's Most Authoritative Guide To Building Your Body. Emmaus, PA: Rodale Books, 2003.

Roizen, Michael F., and Mehmet Oz. You, On A Diet: The Owner's Manual For Waist Management. New York: Free, 2009.

Roizen, Michael F., and Oz, Mehmet. You Staying Young: The Owner's Manual For Extending Your Warranty. New York: Free, 2007.

Making Money And Starting a Business

DeMarco, M. J. The Millionaire Fastlane: Crack The Code to Wealth And Live Rich For A Lifetime! Phoenix, AZ: Viperion, 2011.

Friedman, Nick, Omar Soliman, and Daylle Deanna Schwartz. Effortless Entrepreneur: Work Smart, Play Hard, Make Millions. New York: Three Rivers, 2010.

Mindfulness And Meditation

Kabat-Zinn, Jon. Mindfulness For Beginners: Reclaiming The Present Moment – And Your Life. Louisville, CO: Sounds True, 2011.

Kabat-Zinn, Jon. Wherever You Go, There You Are: Mindfulness Meditation in Everyday Life. New York: Hyperion, 2005.

Popularity

Bennett, Jonathan and David Bennett. Be Popular Now: How Any Man Can Become Confident, Attractive and Successful (And Have Fun Doing It). Lancaster, OH: Theta Hill Press, 2013.

Success Principles

Bandler, Richard. Get The Life You Want: The Secrets To Quick And Lasting Change With Neuro-Linguistic Programming. Deerfield Beach, FL: Health Communications, 2008.

Lieberman, David J. Get Anyone to Do Anything and Never Feel Powerless Again: Psychological Secrets to Predict, Control, and Influence Every Situation. New York: St. Martin's, 2000.

For More Information:

thepopularman.com

Valuable Resources For Shorter Guys:

verticalimpact.net

Consulting And Classes:

thepopularman.com/consulting

Tips Delivered To Your Inbox:

confidencedelivery.com

More Excellent Books

By Theta Hill Press:

thetahillpress.com

Be Popular Now: How Any Man Can Become Confident, Attractive and Successful (And Have Fun Doing It)

Eleven Dating Mistakes Guys Make (And How To Correct Them)

Eleven Dating Mistakes Women Make (And How To Correct Them)

The Teen Popularity Handbook: Make Friends, Get Dates, And Become Bully-Proof

Printed in Great Britain
by Amazon

33845033R00170